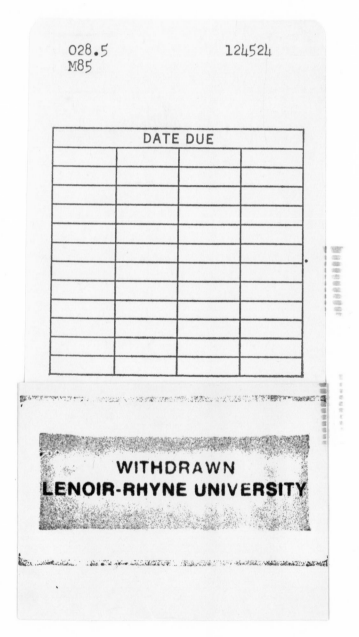

Motivating Children and Young Adults to Read

Motivating Children and Young Adults to Read

Edited with an Introduction by
James L. Thomas and Ruth M. Loring

 ORYX PRESS

Operation Oryx, started more than 15 years ago at the Phoenix Zoo to save the rare white antelope—believed to have inspired the unicorn of mythology—has apparently succeeded. The operation was launched in 1962 when it became evident that the animals were facing extinction in their native habitat of the Arabian peninsula.

An original herd of nine, put together through *Operation Oryx* by five world organizations, now numbers 47 in Phoenix with another 38 at the San Diego Wild Game Farm, and four others which have recently been sent to live in their natural habitat in Jordan.

Also, in what has come to be known as "The Second Law of Return," rare biblical animals are being collected from many countries to roam freely at the Hai Bar Biblical Wildlife Nature Reserve in the Negev, in Israel, the most recent addition being a breeding herd of eight Arabian Oryx. With the addition of these Oryx, their collection of rare biblical animals is complete.

Copyright © 1979 by The Oryx Press
2214 N. Central Avenue at Encanto
Phoenix, AZ 85004

Published simultaneously in Canada

Printed and Bound in the United States of America

Distributed outside North America by
Mansell Publishing
3 Bloomsbury Place
London WC1A 2QA, England
ISBN 0-7201-0932-9

Library of Congress Cataloging in Publication Data

Main Entry under title:

Motivating children and young adults to read.

   Bibliography: p.
   1. Books and reading for children. 2. Books and reading for youth. I. Thomas, James L., 1945-
II. Loring, Ruth M.
Z1037.A1M89   028.5   79-23005
ISBN 0-912700-34-3

Contents

Introduction

All of us who are in some way involved with the education of our young people—whether parents, teachers, or library media specialists—are concerned with preparing these ''soon to be adults'' to function in our society. If there is any reason that the young adult finds this task impossible, it is more than likely a result of his/her inability to read. For a variety of reasons, too many of our young people are graduating into our society and its demands as functional illiterates.

The reality of this sad situation is reported over and over again in U.S. journals and newspapers, and by national and governmental agencies. For example, the Health, Education and Welfare National Advisory Committee on Learning Problems of the U.S. Office of Education recently reported the following findings which pertain to reading:

1. Fifteen percent of the children in [U.S.] schools have severe reading disabilities. This represents an incidence of approximately eight million school children in the United States.

2. The enrollment in the primary and secondary grades of [U.S.] public schools is 51,500,000. The average annual cost per child is $696.00. If one child in twenty (five percent) is not promoted, the national loss expressed in economic terms alone is $1.7 billion.

3. Children of adequate intelligence but retarded in reading often perform adequately in nonreading school work during the early grades. However, as the years of reading failure build up feelings of inadequacy and dissatisfaction with school, these students' overall academic work is severely affected.

4. A follow-up study shows that sixth-grade underachievers continue to be underachievers in the ninth grade, with a resulting tendency to drop out.

5. The American Association of Junior Colleges has estimated that from one-third to one-half of their new students have significant reading problems and that twenty percent of their new students in the most disadvantaged areas are unable to profit from their present remedial programs, so severe is their handicap.

6. Every year some 700,000 children drop out of [U.S.] public school.

7. Sixty percent of the enrollees in the Job Corps Urban Centers have less than a sixth-grade reading ability, and about twenty percent of them read below the third-grade level.

8. Seventy-five percent of juvenile delinquents are significantly retarded in reading. The 1968 cost for detention of a juvenile delinquent in a federal institution was $6935 per year.

9. The retention of reading underachievers costs the [U.S.] public education system in excess of one billion dollars ever year.
10. Unless the causes of failure are determined and specific remedial instruction is provided, a child profits little from repeating the same grade.[1]

The term *reading* can have various meanings. How is the process of reading defined in this book? It is more than a decoding process which involves recognizing or analyzing graphic symbols. Reading is gaining meaning from graphic representations. Reading is a communication skill along with writing, speaking, listening, and thinking. However, reading requires that the communicator be able to decode printed messages into meaningful thoughts. While mere decoding is not reading, it is impossible to read without decoding. Reading should be perceived as the ability possessed by the reader to decode and gain meaning from the written message of the author.

Many readers are nonreaders, not because of an inability to decode or interact, but by choice. Why do some children, young people, and even adults choose not to be readers? There could be many responses to such a question. One of the main reasons is the pressure of time. We live in a world where time is at a premium and there simply exists little time to stop and read. The lack of models is another major reason. Children and young adults do not see adults reading, and therefore they choose not to read. Poor use of available reading materials is also another major factor. Even with school and public libraries for everyone to share, many individuals choose not to use these resources. The influence of media on our daily lives cannot be ignored. By watching television, children are becoming more visually literate than they are print literate. How to motivate able readers to choose to read is the question which concerns teachers, parents, and library media specialists.

Learning to read, or to do anything, is easier when the learning task is meaningful. Carl Rogers points out the importance of this when he states that meaningful learning "has the quality of personal involvement."[2] He also purports that motivation from external sources, such as material rewards, verbal praise, or peer recognition, are effective in learning. However, motivation which comes from within the learner can be more influential in terms of producing behavior and attitude changes which are crucial to becoming a reader. Rogers specifies ten basic principles for learning which effect motivation.

1. Human beings have a natural potentiality for learning.
2. Significant learning takes place when the subject matter is perceived by the student as having relevance for his/her own purposes.
3. Learning which involves a change in self-organization—in the perception of oneself—is threatening and tends to be resisted.

4. Those learnings which are threatening to the self are more easily perceived and assimilated when external threats are at a minimum.

5. When threat to the self is low, experience can be perceived in differentiated fashion and learning can proceed.

6. Much significant learning is acquired through doing.

7. Learning is facilitated when the student participates responsibly in the learning process.

8. Self-initiated learning which involves the whole person of the learner—feelings as well as intellect—is the most lasting and pervasive.

9. Independence, creativity, and self-reliance are all facilitated when self-criticism and self-evaluation are basic and evaluation by others is of secondary importance.

10. The most socially useful learning in the modern world is the learning of the process of learning, a continuing openness to experience and incorporation into oneself of the process of change.[3]

The practitioner concerned with motivating students to read should keep these basic principles in mind as activities and programs are planned and conducted.

In *Motivating Children and Young Adults to Read* we have divided our selection of materials into four main divisions: methodology, interests, programs, and nonprint. In some cases a few of the articles selected could have been placed in more than one of the divisions. Judgment was made by the editors as to the most appropriate location for such articles. Each division is prefaced with an introduction to the articles included. The criteria for selection of the articles were:

1. the article is current: 1973 to present;
2. the author is experienced in the area;
3. the article is written in a readable format;
4. the ideas presented are practicable;
5. the concepts are based on learning theory; and
6. the techniques have proven to be successful.

James L. Thomas and Ruth M. Loring

NOTES

1. C.L. Kline, "The Adolescents with Learning Problems: How Long Must They Wait?" *Journal of Learning Disabilities* 5 (May 1972): 265-66.

2. Carl R. Rogers, *Freedom to Learn* (Columbus, OH: Charles E. Merrill Publishing Co., 1969), p. 5.

3. Ibid., pp. 158-63.

Contributors

Carlene Aborn is Senior Associate, Beckman Associates, Communication Specialists and Consultant for 3M-Wollensak-Mincom Division. "The Newberys: Getting Them Read (It Isn't Easy)" is reprinted by permission of the author. The article originally appeared in the April 15, 1974 issue of *Library Journal*.

J. Estill Alexander, Ed.D., is Professor of Curriculum and Instruction, College of Education, University of Tennessee, Knoxville, TN. "A Child-Based Observation Checklist to Assess Attitudes toward Reading" is reprinted from *Reading Teacher* (April 1978, pp. 769-71) with permission of the authors and the International Reading Association.

David Barber-Smith is Media Program Director at Wordsworth Academy in Fort Washington, PA. He has a B.A. from Harvard University and an Ed.M. in educational media from Temple University. "Use Media to Motivate Reading" is reprinted with permission from *Audiovisual Instruction* (December 1977, pp. 33-34). Copyright © 1977 by the Association for Educational Communications and Technology.

Judith M. Barmore is a fourth grade teacher at Celoron Elementary School in Celoron, NY. "Developing Lifelong Readers in the Middle Schools" originally appeared in *English Journal* (April 1977, pp. 57-61). Copyright © 1977 by the National Council of Teachers of English. Reprinted by permission of the publisher and the authors.

Emmett Albert Betts is Professor Emeritus, University of Miami, Coral Gables, FL. He has over 1400 publications in all areas of reading. "Capture Reading Motivation" is reprinted with permission from *Reading Improvement* (Spring 1976, pp. 41-46). Copyright © 1976 by Project Innovation.

George Canney, Ph.D., is Associate Professor of Reading, Elementary Education, Division of Teacher Education, College of Education, University of Idaho, Moscow, ID. "Commercial Games—Made Relevant for Reading" is reprinted with the author's permission. It was originally printed by the ERIC Documents Reproduction Service, 1976 (ED 131 424).

Ann Carlyle is an elementary school teacher in Golita, CA. She writes curricular materials in the areas of math, outdoor education, and reading. "Comic Book Club: A Collection of Projects for the Comic Cult" is reprinted by special permission of *Learning,* The Magazine for Creative Teaching (April 1978, p. 48). Copyright © 1978 by Education Today Company, Inc., 530 University Avenue, Palo Alto, CA 94301.

Sylvia M. Carter, Ph.D., is Temporary Assistant Professor in the area of reading education at the University of Georgia. She has both taught and consulted in many southwestern states. She is the coauthor with Ira E. Aaron of three books titled *Basics in Reading.* Dr. Carter has conducted extensive research in the area of children's reading interests. "Interests and Reading" is reprinted with permission from the College of Education, University of Georgia from the *Journal of Research and Development in Education,* vol. 11, no. 3 (Winter 1978), Athens, GA, pp. 61-68. Copyright © 1978 by College of Education, University of Georgia.

Jack Cassidy, Ph.D., is Associate Professor of Reading and Gifted Education, Millersville State College, Millersville, PA. He is a member of the IRA Board of Directors and the author of *Basic Life Skills* (Continental Press). He has many years of public school experience in the areas of reading and programs for the gifted. "Survival Reading" is reprinted from the September issue of *Teacher Magazine* with permission of the publisher. This article is copyrighted © 1977 by Macmillan Professional Magazines, Inc. All rights reserved.

Aidan Chambers is an English author and critic. He regularly lectures to teachers and librarians on the subject of children and reading. His latest book is *Breaktime* (Harper), a novel for young adults. He is also the author of *Introducing Books to Children* (Horn Book, Inc.). "Letters from England: Talking about Reading: Back to Basics? (Part I)" is reprinted with permission from *The Horn Book Magazine* (October 1977). Copyright © by The Horn Book, Inc.

Nicholas P. Criscuolo is Supervisor of Reading for the New Haven Public Schools, New Haven, CT. He is the author of eight books and more than 200 journal articles. He is a member of the Board of Directors of the International Reading Association and President of the Connecticut Association for Reading Research. "Reading for Special Occasions" is reprinted by permission from *Learning Today* (Spring 1978, pp. 77-83). Copyright © 1978 by The Library-College Associates, Inc. "Six Simple Crafts for Remedial Reading" is reprinted by permission from *Audiovisual Instruction* (January 1979, pp. 24, 63). Copyright © 1979 by the Association for Educational Communications and Technology.

Joseph M. Cronin is State Superintendent of Education with the Illinois Office of Education. "Send-Home-Sheet" is reprinted from *Instructor* (March 1978, p. 169) and by permission of the State Board of Education, Illinois Office of Education. Copyright © 1978 by The Instructor Publications, Inc.

Mary Eble is Head Library-Media Specialist at Fairview High School and Library-Media Coordinator for the Fairview Park City School District. She is also Adjunct Professor for the School of Library Science at Case Western Reserve University, Cleveland, OH. "Books Unlimited: A School-Wide Reading Program" is reprinted from *Journal of Reading* (November 1978, pp. 123-30) with permission of the authors and the International Reading Association.

Julie P. Johnstone Estes is an instructor in the School of Continuing Education, University of Virginia, Charlottesville, VA. "Twelve Easy Ways to Make Readers Hate Reading (and One Difficult Way to Make Them Love It)" originally appeared in *Language Arts* (November/December 1977, pp. 891-97). Copyright © 1977 by the National Council of Teachers of English. Reprinted by permission of the publisher and the authors.

Thomas H. Estes, Ph.D., is Associate Director of the McGuffey Reading Center of the University of Virginia, Charlottesville, VA. "Twelve Easy Ways to Make Readers Hate Reading (and One Difficult Way to Make Them Love It)" originally appeared in *Language Arts* (November/December 1977, pp. 891-97). Copyright © 1977 by the National Council of Teachers of English. Reprinted by permission of the publisher and the authors.

Arthur Giannini is a teacher in the area of social studies at Block Junior High School in East Chicago, IN. "The Newspaper as a Tool for Teaching Kids to Read," by Ron Soverly, Alex Soverly, Art Giannini, and Walter Matusik is reprinted by permission from *Phi Delta Kappan,* December 1975. Copyright © 1975 by Phi Delta Kappa, Inc.

Betty S. Heathington is currently teaching graduate and undergraduate reading courses in the Reading Center at the University of Maryland, College Park, MD. "A Child-Based Observation Checklist to Assess Attitudes toward Reading" is reprinted from *Reading Teacher* (April 1978, pp. 769-71) with permission of the authors and the International Reading Association.

Nancy Lee is a former graduate assistant in the area of reading methodology at State University College, Fredonia, NY. She taught reading to disadvantaged students in Puerto Rico for a number of years before returning to Holland, NY, where she is now a remedial reading instructor. "Twenty-Five Teacher-Tested Ways to Encourage Voluntary Reading" is reprinted from *Reading Teacher* (October 1973, pp. 48-50) with permission of the authors and the International Reading Association.

Terry C. Ley is Assistant Professor of Secondary Education at Auburn University, Auburn, AL, where he teaches courses in English Education and Secondary Reading. He taught junior and senior high school

English in the Cedar Rapids, IA, schools for 13 years before moving to Alabama in 1974. "Getting Kids Into Books: The Importance of Individualized Reading" is reprinted with permission from *Media & Methods Magazine,* March 1979. Copyright © 1979, North American Publishing Company, Philadelphia, PA. "How to Set Up and Evaluate a DIR Program" is reprinted with permission from *Media & Methods Magazine,* April 1979. Copyright © 1979, North American Publishing Company, Philadelphia, PA.

Ann B. Madison is Acting Principal at Sherwood Forest Elementary School in the Norfolk Public School System, Norfolk, VA. "Read and Rock—A Special Kind of Reading Center" is reprinted from *Reading Teacher* (February 1977, pp. 501-03) with permission of the author and the International Reading Association.

Walter Matusik is Principal of J.L. Block Junior High School in East Chicago, IN. "The Newspaper as a Tool for Teaching Kids to Read," by Ron Soverly, Alex Soverly, Art Giannini, and Walter Matusik is reprinted with permission from *Phi Delta Kappan,* December 1975. Copyright © 1975 by Phi Delta Kappa, Inc.

Philip S. Morse is Associate Professor in the Department of Elementary and Early Childhood Education at the State University of New York College at Fredonia, NY. "Developing Lifelong Readers in the Middle Schools" originally appeared in *English Journal* (April 1977, pp. 57-61). Copyright © 1977 by the National Council of Teachers of English. Reprinted by permission of the publisher and the authors.

Carolyn Paine is a writer and Swap Shop Editor for *Learning* magazine. "If I Read This Book . . . Do I Have to Write a Book Report?" is reprinted by special permission of *Learning,* The Magazine for Creative Teaching, May/June 1978. © 1978 by Education Today Company, Inc., 530 University Avenue, Palo Alto, CA 94301.

Rosemary Lee Potter, Ed.D., is a reading specialist in Clearwater, FL. She is TV TALK columnist for *Teacher Magazine,* TV feature writer for the *St. Petersburg Times,* and author of the book, *New Season: The Positive Use of Commercial Television with Children* (Merrill). "An Interview with a Pioneer" is reprinted from the April issue of *Teacher Magazine* with permission of the publisher. This article is copyrighted © 1978 by Macmillan Professional Magazines, Inc. All rights reserved.

Susan Smith Reilly, Ph.D., is Assistant Professor of Communications at Virginia Polytechnic Institute and State University, Blacksburg, VA. She was Project Director of a Title I Grant to develop audiovisual instructional materials for learning disabled students at Wordsworth Academy. "Use Media to Motivate Reading" is reprinted with permission from *Audiovisual Instruction* (December 1977, pp. 33-34). Copyright © 1977 by the Association for Educational Communications and Technology.

Jeanne Renton is Library-Media Specialist at Fairview Park High School, Fairview Park, OH. "Books Unlimited: A School-Wide Reading Program" is reprinted from *Journal of Reading* (November 1978, pp. 123-30) with permission of the authors and the International Reading Association.

Harold H. Roeder, Ed.D., is Professor of Reading Methods at State University College, Fredonia, NY. Dr. Roeder is interested in motivation and voluntary reading. "Twenty-Five Teacher-Tested Ways to Encourage Voluntary Reading" is reprinted from *Reading Teacher* (October 1973, pp. 48-50) with permission of the authors and the International Reading Association.

Mary June Roggenbuck, Ph.D., is Associate Professor in the Graduate Department of Library and Information Science at The Catholic University of America in Washington, DC. She teaches courses in the areas of media for children and young adults, curricular materials, and the school library media center. She is also published in *Language Arts* and *Horn Book*. "Motivating Farm Children to Read" is reprinted from *Reading Teacher* (May 1977, pp. 868-74) with permission of the author and the International Reading Association.

Wilber S. Slawson is currently Associate Professor of Elementary Education at the University of Tennessee, Knoxville, TN. "Making Home-made Filmstrips" originally appeared in *Language Arts* (February 1976, pp. 125-27). Copyright © 1976 by the National Council of Teachers of English. Reprinted by permission of the publisher and the author.

Alex Soverly is a social studies teacher and Audiovisual Coordinator for Roosevelt High School at East Chicago, IN. "The Newspaper as a Tool for Teaching Kids to Read," by Ron Soverly, Alex Soverly, Art Giannini, and Walter Matusik is reprinted by permission from *Phi Delta Kappan,* December 1975. Copyright © by Phi Delta Kappa, Inc.

Ron Soverly is a social studies teacher at George Washington High School in East Chicago, IN. "The Newspaper as a Tool for Teaching Kids to Read," by Ron Soverly, Alex Soverly, Art Giannini, and Walter Matusik is reprinted by permission from *Phi Delta Kappan,* December 1975. Copyright © 1975 by Phi Delta Kappa, Inc.

Karen Steiner is currently a student in the University of Arkansas' creative writing program. When not teaching English to Arkansas freshman or presenting poetry in the schools at the elementary and secondary levels, she writes. "Child's Play: Games to Teach Reading" is reprinted from *Reading Teacher* (January 1978, pp. 474-77). The article is in the public domain from ERIC/CS, 1111 Kenyon Road, Urbana, IL 61801.

James L. Thomas, Ed.D., is Assistant Professor in the School of Library and Information Sciences at North Texas State University, Denton, TX. "Turning Kids On to Print" is reprinted with permission from *Au-*

George M. Usova, Ph.D., is Education Specialist in the Division of the Disadvantaged for the U.S. Office of Education. Formerly, Dr. Usova was Associate Professor and Coordinator of the Graduate Reading Education Program at The Citadel in Charleston, SC.

Judith Wagner is a free-lance writer who specializes in education and family life. She teaches courses in basic teaching skills and child development at the University of Pittsburgh where she is currently completing her doctorate.

Motivating Children and Young Adults to Read

PART
I

METHODOLOGY

Introduction

Methodology refers to the *how* of motivating students to read. The methods suggested in the following articles are not to be considered as cure-alls but as useful ways to increase motivation. Because motivational techniques vary widely, an attempt has been made to include articles representing a broad spectrum of approaches.

In the article "Twelve Easy Ways to Make Readers Hate Reading (and One Difficult Way to Make Them Love It)," Thomas H. Estes and Julie P. Johnstone suggest that what we teach children to *feel* about reading is more important than teaching them *how* to read. They discuss 12 widely used practices that discourage motivation to read rather than encourage it. Among these are emphases on "reading up to grade level," drilling skills, reading "round robin," and following the manual "to the letter."

Teachers who are actually working with students are in one of the best positions to make recommendations for motivating them. Harold H. Roeder and Nancy Lee surveyed 190 experienced classroom teachers and obtained 300 suggestions of successful techniques. Results of their study are reported in "Twenty-Five Teacher-Tested Ways to Encourage Voluntary Reading."

Sources of reading materials vary widely. The newspaper is one of the most readily available sources. In "The Newspaper as a Tool for Teaching Kids to Read," Alex Soverly and others relate how the newspaper is used to motivate inner-city students in East Chicago to read and to become involved in other curricular activities. After three years of using this technique, they concluded that "the newspaper does motivate students to read. It is up to date; it involves the student reader because his world is right now." Another reading source popular among students is the comic book. In Ann Carlyle's article, "Comic Book Club," she encourages teachers to take advantage of this enthusiasm and lists 20 ideas on how to go about it. In an article representing a different source of reading, Carlene Aborn, a librarian, tells of her experience in using award-winning books to motivate students to read. "The Newberys: Getting Them Read (It Isn't Easy)" reveals the fact that few Newberys would have been read without guidance from the teacher or librarian. Therefore, she urges "if we believe in the value of good books, we will have to give them more than lip service."

Aborn notes that students who are involved in a special program tend to be enthusiastic about it.

Other aspects of methodology appear in George M. Usova's "Techniques for Motivating Interest in Reading for the Disadvantaged High School Student." The author emphasizes the need for special adaptation of techniques for the disadvantaged student; however, his eight suggestions could be applied to the majority of high school students. Mary June Roggenbuck writes of another group of students who have difficulty in relating reading to their daily lives. In "Motivating Farm Children to Read," she examines the stereotyped image of farm life presented in many basal readers. She suggests that teachers must be very selective in choosing a reading series and that they may need to supplement such series with additional trade books and stories more accurately reflecting farm life.

The home is considered as an important factor in the student's success in learning to read. Because television viewing has become such an integral part of the home life, Joseph M. Cronin's ideas have been compiled into a "Send-Home-Sheet" which offers guidelines for viewing and shows how viewing relates to the child's reading. Finally, Aidan Chambers in "Letter from England: Talking about Reading: Back to Basics?" emphasizes that modeling by parents, teachers, and librarians accompanied by exposure to meaningful literature offers the student the best motivation for reading for pleasure and personal growth.

Twelve Easy Ways to Make Readers Hate Reading (and One Difficult Way to Make Them Love It)

by Thomas H. Estes
and Julie P. Johnstone

> Many children, imputing the pain they endured at school to their books . . . so join those ideas together that a book becomes their aversion . . . and their reading becomes a torment to them, which otherwise possibly they might have made the great pleasure of their lives. (John Locke, *An Essay Concerning Human Understanding,* II, xxxiii, 15.)

That statement was published in 1690, though it may have been written any time between 1670 and 1690, the time John Locke took to complete the *Essay* for the first edition. Three hundred years later, the question remains whether children will make reading the great pleasure of their lives.

The way in which we teach reading may easily have an effect on how students feel about reading. Yet almost everything we do in teaching reading is designed basically to teach students *how* to read. Too often, we allow to become incidental the fact that what we do in teaching children how to read does affect how they feel about reading. Surely we should take at least as much care with the effect our teaching may have on students' feelings and predispositions (in short, their attitudes) toward reading as we take with the development of their reading abilities.

No child comes to school intending to hate reading. Rather, most children come to school with high enthusiasm. It is also probably safe to say that no teacher ever does anything with the deliberate intention of making children hate reading. And, for that matter, there are no materials available, nor have there ever been any designed with the intent to cause students to hate reading. Unfortunately, however, the road to bad attitudes is paved with good intentions, and thus it occurred to us that one way to look at attitudes toward reading would be to examine some of what may be done (with all good intentions) to make children hate reading. We will then offer one practice we know to make children love to read.

Each one of the following twelve suggestions has been made to teachers or is official policy of at least some schools. These points are raised not in criticism of teachers or schools, however, since we place unreserved faith in the intentions of both. Rather, we want to raise these points simply to examine them for what they might mean for students' attitudes. It is the love of reading and learning which we take at the outset to be the primary mission of schools. Lacking that accomplishment, any other objective of schools is open to serious question.

Here, then, are our suggestions for how to make children hate reading:

1. *Fail children who do not read up to grade level.* This seems to be a part of the current "back to basics" movement. It is an interesting idea and where practiced it will serve its primary purpose. It will automatically raise the average reading level at every grade. At least until the test-makers have a chance to regroup, it will protect the average from being deflated by the evils of "social promotion." At last we will have passed through the looking glass into a never-never wonderland where all children will be reading above average. Too bad Lewis Carroll didn't think of it for us sooner, but thank heaven for the creativity of some educators and school boards. Alice would have said, "But it's impossible." "No, it's not. We're doing it," the Queen would have replied.

What the Queen fails to realize is that grade level scores on a standardized reading test are derived from the average score of students at a certain grade. The mathematical necessity is that some children will score lower than average, some higher than average on any test of anything—height, weight, color of hair, reading. . . . The mathematical absurdity is that all children could be reading at or above the average for their grade level. But as you recall, the Queen specializes in absurdities.

All we want to ask is, how do you think those children who are sacrificed on the altar of the average score will come to feel about reading? A more reasonable solution to the "problem" of below grade level learners is to teach at any grade level on the level of the needs of the children rather than on the level of the demands of the curriculum.

2. *Define reading ability as scores on a standardized test.* Thus, the object of reading will be to answer questions which follow the reading or to choose a word which could fit into a blank in a sentence and make the best sense by comparison to other choices available. Vocabulary development will be teaching *The Meanings* of words, with a capital *M*; teaching that the dictionary is a compilation of meanings indexed alphabetically.

Reading is not reasonably and logically done for the purpose of answering questions following the reading. Reading most often has as its purpose the answering of questions formulated by the reader before or during reading, and vocabulary development and the meanings of words are as individual as the person to whom the words have meaning in the context in which they are used. The big problem is that in a reasonable and logical sense, reading ability cannot possibly be defined by any standardized test scores. The individual definition which both reading comprehension and vocabulary knowledge must be given is lost in the norm tables. Reading ability, like any other mental ability, defies quantification by means of a standardized test. The risk is that to teach as if standardized test behaviors were valid reading behaviors, to train the behaviors the tests require, is to teach children something about reading which is not true, to waste their time on insipid nonsense when that time could be spent in reading. We wonder how many adults would like to spend their days training to take tests, and whether they wouldn't come to negatively associate what they were doing so that, as Locke warned, reading might become their aversion?

Doris Roettger, a co-author of the *Estes Attitude Scales: Elementary Form* (1976), has collected interview data to get some ideas of why children respond to attitude scale items as they do. In response to the item, "There should be more time for free reading in school," one child among a significant number of others who said similar things, answered, "I agree. But it might not work out because we wouldn't have time to do our worksheets." And, of course, he's right![1]

3. *Drill skills.* This very common practice assumes that learning to read involves the acquisition of a finite but rather large number of relatively distinct and specifiable abilities. There is no shortage of materials available to accomplish this; their names are household words in reading. And do you know what? The materials do work; practically all of them will serve to raise standardized test scores. The materials we're talking about require practice in behaviors almost identical to those required by standardized tests. If it were reasonable and logical to define reading in terms of behaviors required by standardized tests, those materials would teach children how to read. But that's the hitch, the part about reasonable and logical. It's not.

The question which arises is whether we should teach what we think we can measure—the endless lists of skills imagined by reading authorities—or what we think are the strategies characteristic of the fluent reading process? Surely if we choose the latter option, our job becomes more difficult and unspecifiable. But just as surely, the effect of what we do with children will be to create a more realistic view of the reading process and a more positive attitude toward it.

4. *Separate learning to read from reading to learn.* How often have you heard that "in the first three grades children learn to read; from then on they read to learn." In the early grades, there is reading from 10:15 to 10:50

(or some such time) and other things the rest of the day. Children can come to believe that reading is something you do in a reading circle. It is better, we think, to eliminate the reading circle and to institute the discussion circle where the topic is what children have read to learn. The teacher could then help children do what they are naturally trying to do.

A strange thing happened to basal readers on the way to the 70s. Many of today's basals are full of interesting things written by interesting people—real authors. They include things children might read to learn (or, more broadly, might read for literary effect rather than for specific skills development or repetition of words). But the emphasis remains on explicit rules rather than on tacit strategies.

It is more accurate to say that fluent readers employ strategies than apply rules. The learning of explicit rules is neither necessary nor sufficient to the task of learning to read. Quite to the contrary, in fact, the reader needs to develop tacit strategies by practice in reading to learn. Cooper and Petrosky (1976) make this point in their article entitled, "A Psycholinguistic View of the Fluent Reading Process."[2] They list ten strategies which characterize fluent reading. These strategies develop in the context of meaningful reading.

The *Sounds of Language* program by Bill Martin, Jr. and Peggy Brogan (1972) is an example of a basal program which implements a similar view of reading. As those authors say in different ways throughout the program, teaching reading is a matter of providing "opportunities for children to respond to print in naturalistic intuitive ways; [to] release children to verbalizing their intuitive response to language and print, and develop them into word-unlocking skills."[3]

5. Read aloud in groups, round robin. Excursions into classrooms during the reading hour often reveal the familiar scene: a teacher sitting with a group of several children, each stumbling orally and in turn through a sentence or paragraph. This scene is familiar to most of us through our own experience in learning to read, and pervades reading instruction today, even though it is seldom recommended by basal reader manuals. As one teacher said, "If we don't hear them read aloud, we don't know if they are really reading." Someone might ask, though, what the other children in the group are doing while one child is reading aloud. Maybe hoping they won't blunder when it comes their turn? Remember what you were doing? Counting around to see which sentence would be yours and practicing to avoid embarrassment.

One problem with round-robin oral reading is that some children can't or won't keep their place. We recently observed a creative solution: Have children round-robin oral read word-by-word—first child, first word; second child, second word; . . . eighth child, eighth word; first child, ninth word. With expression, please. Ludicrous, you say? But why *more* ludicrous than sentence by sentence or even paragraph by paragraph? Is any of this what reading is, and will kids like reading if they think it is?

Round-robin oral reading is a technique for teaching oral reading involving the precise pronunciation of each word. Kenneth Goodman (1973) distinguishes "recoding" (moving from the graphic code to the oral code) from "decoding" (moving from the graphic code to meaning with no intervening pronunciation). As he says, "I have encountered many youngsters who are so busy matching letters to sounds and naming word shapes that they have no sense of the meaning of what they are reading."[4] Pronouncing words is a process quite different from getting meaning. The surprising thing to some may be that the two processes may actually interfere with one another!

6. *Insist on careful reading for detail.* The problem is, we don't remember details or words. The mind does not often *recall* from memory. It constructs ideas in response to how what has been read affects the reader. F.C. Bartlett made this point in 1932 in a book entitled *Remembering:*

> When a subject is being asked to remember, very often the first thing that emerges is something of the nature of the attitude. The recall is then a construction, made largely on the basis of this attitude, and its general effect is that of a justification of the attitude.[5]

The construction of ideas depends on an attitude toward (more generally, a *feel* for) the author's message. It is quite possible that overly careful reading could interfere with comprehension since the attempt to remember detail is often at the expense of general understanding. Analogously, if listeners attend to every word in speech in an attempt to remember words rather than meanings, they will often miss the speaker's point. If they listen only for the point of the message, however, they can easily fill in detail with surprising accuracy.

Children fall into the habit of reading for precise recall when they are asked to answer every question at the ends of reading selections. Trying to remember details overcomes a natural tendency to process ideas. Ostensibly, at least, the purpose of detailed questions is to generate discussion. But either good discussion of a story grows naturally out of excitement generated by the reading *or* the discussion is unnatural and stilted, a bore and a punishment for reading.

Last Christmas, the first author read to his students a story by Truman Capote called, "A Christmas Memory." It is beautiful and poignant, as affecting as any story one could choose. Many of the students cried at the end. Their teacher looked at the questions following the story—he cried.

1. To what uses is the dilapidated baby carriage put in the various seasons?
2. What evidence is there in the story that the setting, a rural town, is located in the southern area of our country?

Ad Nauseum.

7. *Follow the lesson plan in the manual to the letter*. In recent basal manuals something called *anticipated responses* is highlighted—what the child is to say. Why not simplify the whole thing by giving the children their script, we take ours, and all play out each scenario in order?

Facetious? Sure. The question here is not manual versus no manual, but rather, whether the teacher's eyes should be on the children and what they're trying to do rather than on the manual and what it says to do. The paradox is that by trying to make the job easier, manuals may make it impossible.

8. *Don't skip stories in the basal, and do not switch children from one basal series to another*. If you skip stories, you'll skip skills and get into vocabulary which is too difficult for the children. If you use more than one basal reader at one time, you'll surely play havoc with the systematic sequence of skills development and vocabulary control. Tinker and McCullough (1952, 1962, 1968, 1975) and others have made this point a part of conventional wisdom:

> Basic reading materials should foster continuity in reading development so that there will be no gaps in a child's reading experience. [One risk is that] children switched from one basic series to another are confronted with different sequences in building vocabulary and other skills.[6]

Two problems arise here. In the first place, there is no sequence of skills and no necessity for artificial control and repetition of vocabulary in basal readers. Not one shred of evidence exists to suggest the necessity or existence of either, outside a basal reader or the mind of a basal reader writer. The fact that no two reading programs follow the same sequence of vocabulary development or other skills is evidence that no such sequence exists. A child's exposure to a word or skill in a basal series is no guarantee of mastery. Concomitantly, there are many children who have achieved mastery far beyond the level of the basal to which they are assigned in school.

In the second place, there is the question of whether children's interest and curiosity in reading to learn is to have more credence and force than the artificial need to keep the child "locked in" the sequential steps of skill development.

9. *For vocabulary development, have children copy definitions from the dictionary*.

> "Bitzer," said Thomas Gradgrind, "your definition of a horse."

> "Quadruped. Gramnivorous. Forty teeth, namely twenty-four grinders, four eye-teeth, and twelve incisive. Sheds coat in spring; in marshy countries sheds hoofs too. Hoofs hard, but requiring to be shod with iron. Age known by marks in mouth. . . ."

"Now girl number twenty," said Mr. Gradgrind, "you know what a horse is."

—Charles Dickens, *Hard Times*

In what sense, if any, can Girl Number Twenty be said to "know what a horse is"? Yet Bitzer's definition is quite precise, like many found in dictionaries. What is the problem? We think it is that dictionaries do not list meanings at all, they list definitions, and there is a difference. Bitzer did not say what "horse" means; he defined the word. Words *come to mean* in the minds of those for whom they have meaning, and those meanings are unique. Words do not mean independently of someone to whom they mean. Vocabulary development, the development of a rich store of meaningful words for expression in language, is the development of meanings in the sense we're using the term. It is direct and purposeful, personal and stimulating, marked by curiosity and inquiry. It is not as much an activity as a way of thinking about language and communication. To substitute for this the endless lists of words to be found in dictionaries, their definitions copied but soon forgotten, is contrary to the essential purpose of vocabulary development. That purpose, we might say, is the enhancement of the natural curiosity about language. Curiosity is fragile, though, and if it is killed, students often resent it without knowing why. All they do know is that *vocabulary development* is no longer interesting. No wonder at that.

10. *Do not let children read ahead in the story to find out how it is organized or told.* It is as if to anticipate what is coming will spoil it. Yet to have an idea of what is coming is to have a general idea which the details will confirm, which will give meaning to the whole. How many adult readers feel guilty for looking ahead, for reading the conclusion of even a research article, let alone a Poe mystery. There is no formula for reading, most certainly, any more than there is a formula for any kind of communication. But most assuredly, reading does not begin with word one and end with word last. To teach it as if it did runs counter to the grain of good sense and, again, teaches children that reading is something it is not.

11. *Do not have ungraded materials around, like paperback books, magazines, or newspapers.* Daniel Fader's experience (1968, 1971) suggested that those were the only things that children who hated reading would read.[7, 8] But what about the skills? What about vocabulary control? What about them? Law (1977) asked dozens of questions of remedial reading students in an attempt to find out what causes attitudes toward reading to change. The clearest factor responsible for positive attitude change in those reluctant readers' minds was *prominently displayed paperback books*. This factor distinguished children who had come to like reading from those who continued to dislike it.[9]

12. *Always set children's purposes for them.* Quoting again from Bartlett:

> It is fitting to speak of every human cognitive (activity) as an *effort after meaning.* . . . When we try to discover how this is done we find that always it is by an effort to connect what is given with something else.[10]

Having a personal purpose for reading which leads to a connection between something in the reader's mind to something in the writer's message, that's the game. We can comprehend only that which we can relate; we can relate only that which we know. Thus, purpose for reading is as personal as thought.

The job of the teacher in directing children's efforts to read is to help them raise to consciousness what they know which will relate to what they are learning. By thought-provoking questions asked, by the connections suggested, by the anticipation which is built as a foundation on which understandings are set, the teacher helps readers set purposes for themselves.

And, finally, here is one difficult way to make children love reading: Be as certain as you possibly can be that anything you ask any student to read is something he or she can read and will want to read.

Samuel Johnson said in 1763, "A man ought to read just as inclination leads him; for what he reads as a task will do him little good."

William Dean Howells made the same point in 1895: "The book which you read from a sense of duty, or because for any reason you must, does not commonly make friends with you."

Children must come to see reading as something *they* do, rather than as a task imposed on them. Students control their learning, inevitably; the teacher can only serve to *facilitate* learning, making children free to learn in the hope that they will love it. Then may reading become for them the great pleasure of their lives, and may what we do become worth the difficult job it is.

NOTES

1. T. H. Estes et al., *Estes Attitude Scales: Elementary Form* (Charlottesville, VA: Virginia Research Associates, 1976).

2. C. R. Cooper and A. R. Petrosky, "A Psycholinguistic View of the Fluent Reading Process," *Journal of Reading* 20 (1976): 184-207.

3. B. Martin and P. Brogan, *Sounds of Language*, teacher's ed. (New York: Holt, Rinehart, Winston, 1972), p. 11.

4. K. Goodman, "Psycholinguistic Universals in the Reading Process," in *Psycholinguistics and Reading*, ed. F. Smith (New York: Holt, Rinehart, Winston, 1973), p. 26.

5. F. C. Bartlett, *Remembering* (London: Cambridge University Press, 1932), p. 207.

6. M. A. Tinker and C. M. McCullough, *Teaching Elementary Reading* (Englewood Cliffs, NJ: Prentice-Hall, 1952, 1962, 1968, 1975).

7. D. N. Fader and E. B. McNeil, *Hooked on Books: Program and Proof* (New York: Putnam, 1968).

8. D. Fader, *The Naked Children* (New York: Macmillan, 1971).

9. L. D. Law, "An Exploratory Field Study Concerning the Factors in Reading Attitude Change" (Ph.D. diss., University of Virginia, 1977).

10. Bartlett, *Remembering*, p. 44.

REFERENCES

Spache, G.D., and Spache, E.B. *Reading in the Elementary School.* Boston: Allyn & Bacon, 1977.

Smith, F. "Twelve Easy Ways to Make Learning to Read Difficult." In *Psycholinguistics and Reading,* edited by F. Smith. New York: Holt, Rinehart, Winston, 1973.

Twenty-Five Teacher-Tested Ways to Encourage Voluntary Reading

by Harold H. Roeder
and Nancy Lee

Motivating children to read for their own enjoyment is a major objective of reading instruction at all levels. Unfortunately, many teachers soon discover that this is by no means an easy task; it requires a great deal of originality, energy, and careful planning. Since a glib and somewhat creative author or college professor can effortlessly list numerous ways of motivating students to read for their own enjoyment, textbooks and journals abound with suggestions which purport to encourage voluntary reading.

However, which suggestions actually work? In an effort to answer this question, the authors conducted a survey. Succinctly stated, the major purpose of this investigation was to ascertain which techniques teachers have found to be most effective in encouraging students to read for their own enjoyment.

The sample comprised 190 experienced classroom teachers. The subjects were enrolled in randomly selected graduate education courses which were being taught at three different teacher education institutions in the state of New York. The subjects represented a variety of instructional levels which included primary, intermediate, secondary, college, and special education. Teaching experience of the subjects ranged from less than one year to more than 25 years of classroom experience.

The sample included both males and females. Subjects ranged from 21 to over 50 years of age.

The semi-structured questionnaire had been pretested and revised accordingly. The questionnaires were administered during classtime. Of the 190 subjects who were surveyed, 8 reported that because of the uniqueness of their particular professional assignments (school administrator, guidance counselor, and so on) the instrument could not be completed.

ANALYSIS OF DATA

The subjects listed approximately 300 suggestions which they found to be successful in encouraging students to undertake voluntary reading activity. In an effort to assist teachers who are interested in motivating students to read, the following list of "Twenty-Five Teacher-Tested Ways to Encourage Voluntary Reading" was compiled. The criteria established for evaluating each of the original suggestions: a) frequency of response; b) apparent success of the suggestion as indicated by the respondent; c) originality and uniqueness of the suggestion.

In view of the fact that interest in reading can be, and should be, highly infectious and extremely contagious, the authors would like to guarantee that prolonged use of the accompanying list will result in a reading epidemic. Unfortunately, such a guarantee cannot be made. However, if you and your class are suffering from a case of the "reading blahs," the authors recommend the following procedures: take two suggestions, get lots of books, and exude enthusiasm.

If your condition does not begin to improve within just ten days, see your reading teacher.

Twenty-Five Teacher-Tested Ways to Encourage Voluntary Reading

Pri.	Inter.	Sec.	Suggested levels
1. x	x		*Auction.* "Auction" paperbacks brought in by students. Let children bid with play money. Use student auctioneers who encourage bidding.
2.	x	x	*Teacher interest.* Frequently ask students, "What have you been reading lately?" "Read anything interesting over the weekend?" Keep up with what they are reading.
3. x	x		*Read to the kindergarten.* Have primary and elementary level students take turns reading books to small groups of kindergarten children.
4. x	x	x	*Awards.* Students who have read a specific number of books receive an award, for example, "The 5 Book Award."
5. x	x		*Read-in.* Have each child select a partner and set aside specific times for partners to read to each other.
6.	x	x	*Promotional campaign.* Stage a sales campaign for promoting books. Students can act like advertising executives and "sell" books.

Pri.	Inter.	Sec.	Suggested levels, cont'd.

7. x   x   *Topic of the month.* Colorful posters can be made to advertise a specific topic for each month, such as "nature stories."

8.   x   x   *Critical reading.* Do a unit on the criteria for evaluating a book. Encourage students to find examples in their own reading.

9. x   x   *Tapes of books.* Have children tape record sections of a book or situations from a book. Develop a game, such as "Which book did this passage come from?" or "I'm thinking of a book in which a character said _____."

10.   x   x   *Quotations.* Use direct quotations from famous figures in history on the value of books. Mount them in conspicuous places around your classroom. Change frequently.

11. x   x   *Series.* Encourage students to read a book from a series, or to read a book by an author who has written several similar books.

12. x   x   x   *Home library.* Encourage students to start libraries of their own. Help get them started with a list of "musts."

13. x   x   x   *Write books.* Have children write, illustrate, and bind their own books. Encourage "pen" names. Circulate the books around the classroom and, if possible, the school.

14. x   x   x   *Bookclubs.* Form a classroom book club with specific book reading quotas and activities for members.

15. x   x   *Bulletin boards.* For example, "Books for Athletes," "Good Books for Girls," "Animal Books."

16. x   x   x   *Library corner.* Partition off part of the classroom with a screen and load it with a variety of books, magazines and newspapers. Provide students with time to use the library corner.

17. x   x   x   *Read to children.* Read students brief but complete stories as often as possible. Provide variety—high interest, humor, special interest, timely.

18. x   x   *Stop at exciting point.* Read orally from a book and stop at the most exciting point. (Have several copies available.)

19. x   x   *Thought-provoking objects.* Bring in thought-provoking objects which will lead students to read books on specific topics.

20.   x   x   *Community members.* Invite members of the community to speak to the class on their special interests. Be certain to provide a link between the presentation and the reading activity.

Pri.	Inter.	Sec.	Suggested levels, cont'd.
21. x	x	x	*Books from home.* Bring in your own books from home and "talk them up."
22. x	x		*Paraphrase books.* Using their own works, have students retell stories which they have read. Encourage interested children to read the book.
23. x	x		*Puppet show.* Have children make up puppet shows based on books which they have read.
24. x	x	x	*Role playing.* Create enthusiasm through plays and acting out the dialogue in books.
25. x	x	x	*Exude enthusiasm.* Above all, display a positive, enthusiastic attitude toward reading.

The Newspaper as a Tool for Teaching Kids to Read

by Ron Soverly, Alex Soverly,
Art Giannini, and Walter Matusik

Thousands of school kids in America have never really learned to read. At Block Junior High School in East Chicago, Indiana, we found not an absolute answer to the reading problem, but a tool which all teachers can use. The possibilities for students are limitless. The tool is the daily newspaper.

By the time many students get to Block, they have suffered years of embarrassment and frustration resulting from minimal reading skills. They have no desire to open a book. They will not. If pushed into doing so, they will completely turn off the teacher.

However, for the last three years, students at Block have been receiving each morning one of Chicago's major newspapers with such growing eagerness that, last year, 350 students (all of those involved in the team-taught U.S. history classes) were getting a morning paper.

At the beginning of each school year, students (and their parents) are told why they should receive a paper. In simple terms, the teachers suggest the idea of keeping abreast of current events and outline how the newspaper is to be used. Students are given time to read the paper in class; study guides, lectures, group projects, and small quizzes all come directly from each morning's paper. Students are not required to take the paper (there are always extras in the room), but all are encouraged to buy one for a nickel a day, or one dollar a month. To make the bookkeeping easier, money is collected on a monthly basis; each student has 60 days to pay his/her bill. The students are completely responsible for distributing the papers.

Every student is urged to take the paper home each day to encourage family participation. We do this because in many homes there is no reading material; communication between the student and his/her parents (who at times have a hostile attitude toward the schools) often opens up when they sit and talk about the day's news. Both the family and the child become involved.

For about the first two weeks, we do nothing with the paper except give the students ten minutes to look through it. We don't tell them what to read or why. If a student spends the time just going through the comics or sports pages, it doesn't matter, because the student is *reading*. The more an individual reads, no matter what the subject, the better reader s/he can become. Curiosity will help keep him/her reading.

Students soon begin to see reasons for reading other sections besides sports and the comics. Even the working of crossword puzzles by these students represents a positive improvement. Teachers hand out study guides which cover every section of the newspaper. The purpose and benefits to be derived from each section are listed.

Group work is very important when working with the newspaper. Even in the beginning, students eagerly discuss why a basketball team is better, why a player should try to be better even when s/he's at the top, or how a comic strip character could have gotten himself/herself out of trouble. The students are no longer just seeing facts and forgetting them— they are *reading* and becoming involved with what they read. It is a learning process—something that these kids have only observed, not shared.

Positive results tend to appear first among the girls. Usually the paper carries a weekly (sometimes daily) section dealing with foods or fashion. The girls love trying out hair styles and give our home economics department headaches by experimenting with different recipes. In time, they go beyond the paper and spend many hours in the library getting books on fashion, foods, and the women's movement. We encourage this by asking for in-class presentations on new fads or tryouts of new recipes with the entire class sampling them.

Involvement with the newspaper increased greatly during the first year of the project. Besides the classroom work, the kids started projects that involved their parents. During National Fire Prevention Week, which was covered in feature stories and news articles by the papers, the students worked on a fire-prevention checklist using information from the newspaper. At home, with their parents, they looked for and corrected any dangers which they saw in their own homes or apartments. Some students who lived in multifamily dwellings succeeded in lobbying for improvements that benefited everyone in the building.

Most major newspaper programs have free supplemental materials to help the teacher do more on specific subjects. The *Chicago Tribune* has an excellent collection of background reports on over 90 topics. These reports are supplied free each week to every child in the program.

One unit based on this material proved to be a success for both teachers and students. Since our school contains roughly equal proportions of two ethnic groups, two separate lesson plans were created—one on the history and present role of the Negro in America, the other on the Latino in America. Each student received separate background reports on the subjects, together with study guides, puzzles, films, and filmstrips. Guest speakers were brought in to talk about being Black or Brown, or about the attitudes of Whites in America. Group projects were also set up; each group contained both Black and Latino students.

In two weeks the Black and the Brown students had begun to understand not only themselves but their classmates as well. Many of the Black students said that, for the first time, they saw that they had many things in common with their Latin friends, that they shared many of the same problems. Although the Latino students did comment on their language problems, they too saw problems that were not just theirs but were shared by all minorities in America. Contributions by all groups were brought out in the open and discussed. The students were made more conscious of their peers of different ethnic backgrounds.

All during the first year, the students were learning to dig for information, to learn on their own. Heretofore, even the sight of a textbook discouraged many boys and girls. With the newspaper, not only did they look on their own, but they started to ask questions and go to the library for more information. Needless to say, we tried to correlate their efforts with their schoolwork; the newspaper served as a step to improvement in many areas—especially reading.

Once the program was well under way, the students took field trips to different newspapers and saw—from the cutting of the tree to the finished product—how a newspaper ends up in the hands of the reader. We scheduled other trips that helped the students understand certain subject material in the textbooks and the newspaper. For example, in conjunction with a unit on the American Indian, our students visited a museum which had on exhibit items from various Indian tribes. Teachers in the building were encouraged not only to take these trips with their students but to use the newspaper to help them with lesson plans—no matter what the subject.

After three years of using the newspaper in history classrooms, we have formed many conclusions. The newspaper *does* motivate a student to read. It is up to date; it involves the student reader because his/her world is right now. The variety piques his/her curiosity and fuels his/her interest. Many of our poorer students, who had refused to read anything, turned into avid readers.

Group participation in class improved beyond all expectations. Students at times fought with each other just for the chance to contribute to class discussion on that day's newspaper topics. Awareness of the problems of our society, relations between different races, and the importance of knowing enough to hold down a job and to be a good citizen—all were brought into the open through involvement in the paper.

Student interest was keener, with better communication opening up between students and teachers. While students' grades did not shoot up in other classes because of the newspaper, many teachers reported greater participation in class discussion. Some of the slower students went to the school or city libraries for the first time in their lives to search for information.

As involvement with the newspaper increased, boys and girls who subscribed to the paper were convincing their friends and classmates of the advantages of reading a newspaper; such student testimonials produced many more subscriptions.

Our students seemed to thrive on the freedom to choose what they read and to draw their own conclusions. They felt *involved*, not just with school but with the community and the nation.

If we, as educators, could only carry this interest into all parts of the learning experience, we would have a powerful motivating tool. The newspaper is the textbook of tomorrow. Why not use it today to build a better future?

Comic Book Club: A Collection of Projects for the Comics Cult

by Ann Carlyle

We're a country of joiners, with organizations for every interest. If your kids are hooked on comic books, you might suggest a comic book club—for the greater enjoyment of comics and integration of comics into many phases of the curriculum.

Club members are responsible for starting a club library of comics. If each member is able to bring in three to five comic books, that should get the club off to a good start.

Members may read comics during their free time, and one day a week comics become the regular fare for their reading classes. One enjoyable way of using comics is for each reader to take a character and read that character's speech balloons aloud, following along in the story sequence. (The comic-book format is perfect for this sort of "reader's theater" production.)

Each member of the comic book club is required to complete one special project a week to retain membership. Here is a list of suggestions:

1. Make a poster for your favorite character. (An opaque projector can be useful here.)

2. Write 10 facts about your favorite character.

3. Pretend your character is in our class. Write about one day's happenings. Include conversations with your character.

4. Write a list of 10 things you might find in the top drawer of your favorite character's dresser.

5. Find out when your character was first drawn. Find out about the artist and creator.

6. Trace a page out of a comic book, but leave off the words in the speech balloons. Prepare the page for duplication on a ditto master. See what other students put in the balloons. (Make your own version of what goes in the balloons too.)

7. Make hand puppets or papier-mâché figures that are comic characters.

8. Make a costume for one of the figures you made in Project 7.

9. Arrange an unlikely meeting of two characters from different comics, and write their conversation.

10. Create a family tree or name the relatives of some comic character.

11. Write a letter to the editor of a comic book. Ask for questions to be included in the letter.

12. Make a comic-character word-search maze for fellow club members to solve.

13. Make a list of 10 to 15 exclamations and sound-effect words used in comics.

14. Make a glossary of symbols in comics.

15. Find and list 10 words that are new to you. Find and write their definitions.

16. Survey other members on their favorite characters. Graph the data.

17. Survey other members on the number of comics they have. Graph the data.

18. Graph the number of times something violent happens in the first 10 pages of several different comic books. (Count kicks, shoves, punches, etc.)

19. List commercial products that use comic characters in advertising.

20. Decorate a notebook or other useful item with comic characters.

This is a club that should thrive even without a president, regular meetings or a secret handshake—but such elements can be added if the comic club membership stops reading long enough to vote.

The Newberys: Getting Them Read (It Isn't Easy)

Once again, I found myself staring at that group of books which held the most coveted award in the field of children's literature: the John Newbery Medal. Although they were award winning books, they certainly had not, in the first two months of school, found their way into the arms of eager-to-read students. I had carefully scrutinized the charge-out statistics for these books and found them appalling. Many of the Newbery books had never been taken off the shelf. Some that did enjoy a certain popularity were *Rabbit Hill* by Robert Lawson (Viking, 1944), *Call It Courage* by Armstrong Sperry (Macmillan, 1940), *Island of the Blue Dolphins* by Scott O'Dell (Houghton, 1960), *The Matchlock Gun* by Walter D. Edmonds (Dodd, 1941), and *It's Like This, Cat* by Emily C. Neville (Harper, 1963). Much of their popularity stemmed from the fact that these books had been read aloud by teachers which, in turn, stimulated the students to read them.

One book in particular whose lack of use really astounded me was *Amos Fortune, Free Man* by Elizabeth Yates (Dutton, 1967). Until two years ago, Melrose Elementary School in Pinellas County, Florida had a totally Black student enrollment, and during those years there was not much quality Black oriented literature available. Yet *Amos Fortune*, purchased in 1962 [sic], had never been read.

The Newbery award books had been a bone of contention with me ever since I had become involved in children's literature. Many questions arose in my mind concerning these books. Were they truly the best in children's literature? If so, why weren't they being read? What would it take to make the students want to read them? If the students were exposed to them, would they continue to read quality books or would they revert back to the more popular books? As the questions kept popping up, I recalled something May Hill Arbuthnot once wrote: "A book is a good book for children only when they enjoy it; a book is a poor book for children even when adults rate it a classic if children are unable to read it or are bored by its contents." If this is true, then most of the Newberys would fall into the category of "poor" for when students enjoy a book, that book's popularity spreads like wildfire. Unfortunately, this wasn't exactly the case with a number of these books.

I decided to take some action and formulate a literature program revolving around these books to solve this problem. Time was to be my greatest obstacle. As I was the sole media specialist and had only student assistants, the time I could spend on this endeavor would not be enough for an in-depth project, but I decided I would try for a capsule program rather than do nothing at all. With the approval of Mr. Sokolowski, who taught accelerated language arts, and my principal, Sally Davis, I immediately began to plan.

I ordered all the available sound filmstrips and recordings from Miller-Brody Productions and Viking Recordings. I re-read all the books so that I would have a working knowledge of each, developed a short history of the Newbery award, criteria for judging a book, questions to consider in reading a book, and an annotated list of the Newberys. Horn Book publications and other reliable books were used as a source of annotations. A list of enriching and creative activities was compiled in conjunction with each book.

At the first class meeting we discussed the entire program at length, and I distributed all the materials I had gathered. The following requirements and procedures were agreed upon by a large majority of the students.

1. Participation in the program would be voluntary. Those not interested would be able to do their regular classroom work providing it did not interfere with others.

2. For each book read, a card containing a brief annotation and a critical opinion was to be turned in. (I had stressed during the discussion that I wanted honest opinions about each book and that the important point was *why* they reached a favorable or unfavorable conclusion. I also had made it clear that if they started a book and decided they didn't like it, they were not required to finish it. However, it had been suggested that they read at least two chapters before making a decision.)

3. When they had read at least ten Newbery award books, they would become members of the Newbery Award Club, receiving buttons and membership cards.

4. Classes would be conducted for one and a half hours a week, and smaller groups and projects would be scheduled as needed.

5. A chart of the Newbery books was to be made, and as each student finished a book, he or she would initial a given area. This would provide us with an easy, visual method of seeing which books were being read and which were the most popular.

By the end of the period it was apparent that these students felt honored to have been selected for a special program and were most eager to cooperate. I felt that a good beginning had been made. Nearly all of the

Newberys were charged out in the next few minutes, and I could hardly wait for the reactions.

In a matter of two days, student review cards began coming in; comments about books were being exchanged; and more Newbery award books were going out. During weekly classes, we would listen to a recording or see a sound filmstrip and listen to various students' reactions to books they were reading. These sessions were exciting, and the interaction was keen. Many times when students said they hadn't enjoyed a particular book, comments from other students who had spurred them on to try the book again, and often they were favorably impressed the second time around.

It became very obvious that the recordings and filmstrips did much to stimulate interest in a book, as did favorable comments from the peer group. I was impressed with the quality of the material and used the accompanying vocabulary lists and suggested activities.

We were really gathering steam now, and as soon as five or more students had read the same book, we held small group discussions in the media center. These rap sessions provided one of the highlights of the project. The first book we discussed was *Summer of the Swans* by Betsy Byars (Viking, 1970). All those in the group had reacted favorably to this book. We talked about mental retardation and emotional problems, the students' feelings concerning what it would be like to have a mentally retarded person in the family, and what he or she could do to help people in similar situations. The students were perceptive, their ideas fresh and provocative, their questions and comments right to the point. The contemporary theme and the humor and realism of *Summer of the Swans* really captured the interest of the group. The students and I discovered that sharing opinions about books can be a meaningful learning experience.

Taking the class to the film *Sounder*, based on the Newbery award winning book by William H. Armstrong (Harper, 1962), was an experience. These youngsters were severe critics. They proceeded to tear the movie apart as soon as it was over. We had the liveliest discussion while waiting for their parents to take them home.

The majority of students who had read the book were terribly disappointed in the movie. Their reasons varied, but most felt that the movie was not true to the book and that much of the dramatic impact was lost when the boy's father did not die. They couldn't understand why scenes such as the baseball game had been added when it didn't add anything of importance to the story. They had now had their first experience with an adaptation of a book for the screen and, without exception, they all agreed that the book outshone the movie.

The class had a similar reaction after watching Walt Disney's adaptation of *Call It Courage*.

Numerous other activities were being pursued along the way. Book jackets were designed and used to promote interest in particular books. Students read or dramatized incidents from their favorite books. "Newbery I.Q. Tests" taken from *Elementary English* were given. Papers were written on authors of other topics that were selected, and all the while the cards kept pouring in and more and more students became members of the Newbery Club.

In the meantime, I was savoring the comments on their cards, which I found to be spontaneous, perceptive, and honest:

• About *The Cat Who Went to Heaven* by Elizabeth Coatsworth (Macmillan, 1967) one boy wrote, "I didn't like it. It was not exciting or interesting, and the language was stilted." Many others voiced the same sentiment about this book. Only a few enjoyed it.

• *Summer of the Swans* evoked these comments: "I liked it because it shows how real life is and how we react to different things." "I liked this book a great deal because it tells about a girl who feels sorry for herself and, at the end of the story, she realizes how ignorant she had been for having so much self-pity." "It was a good book, and I think it was pretty funny when she said she had duck feet." "I liked this story because it was full of excitement . . . I felt as though I was Sarah."

• About *Amos Fortune, Free Man*, these were written: "This has been my favorite Newbery." "I loved this book very much, especially how Amos managed to give others their freedom." "I liked the book because things like that really happened."

• A boy, having read *Sounder* twice, commented, "I loved it, it's the best book I ever read in my whole life."

• Students, on the whole, commented unfavorably about *Strawberry Girl* by Lois Lenski (Lippincott, 1945): "It was boring to me, but it might not be to others. It didn't suit me." "I didn't like the language they used. It is not a very good book to read."

Every book read had both good and bad comments, and it became apparent that the books favored were those that had meaningful themes and relevancy to the students' lives. These books also contained humor, excitement, fantasy, pathos, and realism in a manner which the students enjoyed. Books with difficult names, foreign settings, lengthy descriptive passages, and colloquial language did not appeal to a majority of the readers.

As another activity I borrowed a copy of *Julie of the Wolves* by Jean Craighead George (Harper, 1972) from our County Media Center and each day read it aloud to the class for half an hour.

They were a responsive audience, and the drama, natural history details, and reality of the story held their interest. When I had finished the book, they wrote critical essays about Julie and her situation. One thought permeated all the papers: Julie was an amazingly brave girl, and most of the students felt that they would not have survived a similar predicament. Without exception, they felt that the book had great value.

During one of our classroom discussions a student suggested that perhaps we could have one large, creative group project as a culminating activity. After some ideas had been considered, it was decided that we would create a yarn-on-burlap tapestry. For each Newbery book a symbol was designed and then drawn on the burlap. In the center of the tapestry was a facsimile of the John Newbery Medal. All of the symbols and the Medal were stitched in bright colors.

The stitchery was done with great care by small groups composed mainly of boys. Whenever they had free time they would come to the Media Center and work on the tapestry. It was truly a work of love, and when completed it was beautiful. The class was proud of it. We unveiled it during the Sixth Grade Awards Night Program, and the response from the audience was most rewarding to those who had worked so hard to produce this tribute to the Newbery Medal Book Program. The class later presented the tapestry to the school as a farewell gift. It hangs in the cafeteria for all to enjoy.

In the final analysis, I would have to say that not all of my questions concerning the readability of the Newbery award books were answered, but I was able to draw some tentative conclusions:

1. This student group did not consider all of the Newbery books as the best in children's literature. There were a few that they felt did not deserve an award. The results of a preference survey showed that the most popular book was *Summer of the Swans* and the least popular was *The Trumpeter of Krakow* by Eric P. Kelly (Macmillan, 1966).

2. Audiovisual experiences tended to promote greater interest in a book.

3. Peer acceptance of a given book stimulated interest and encouraged others to read it.

4. Few of the Newbery books would ever be read without strong direction and enthusiasm from a teacher or librarian. (To further substantiate this premise, I checked the charge-out statistics in two other elementary schools and a junior high and found that most of the books were not being read elsewhere either.)

5. In general, students who are a part of a special program tend to cooperate and display an ethusiasm generally not found in their normal classroom attitudes.

Did the students enjoy the program? This question was best answered when, on Awards Night, a top student was enumerating all the wonderful and special activities his class had enjoyed while at Melrose in his farewell address. Along with the picnics, the trip to Disneyworld, and excursions to Busch Gardens, the Newbery awards program was given recognition.

My involvement in this program was most rewarding and though I still question some of the Newbery awards, I have come away with some thoughts concerning our roles as media specialists. If we believe in the value of good books, we will have to give them more than lip service. We need to read more and become truly knowledgeable about the books that are turning our young people on, so that we can suggest a quality book in the area of their reading choice. Our school systems will have to provide media specialists with time and clerical help so that we are free to do the type of job we are best suited for—that of inciting students to read and appreciate good literature.

SOURCE MATERIALS

How Book Papers. Volume 1. Toronto: How Book, 1955.

Miller, Bertha Mahoney, and Field, Eleanor Whitney, eds. *Newbery Medal Books 1922-1955*. Boston: Horn, 1955.

For a complete listing of Newbery sound filmstrips, records, and other materials write to: Miller-Brody Productions, Inc., 342 Madison Ave., New York, NY 10017.

For a catalog of recorded books write to: Viking Press, Audiovisual Dept., 625 Madison Ave., New York, NY 10022.

Techniques for Motivating Interest in Reading for the Disadvantaged High School Student

by George M. Usova

One of the chief problems secondary school teachers encounter is that of motivating the disadvantaged youth to read. In-class reading and out-of-class reading assignments become an almost daily battle and struggle between teacher and students. This despairing situation often leads the teacher into abandoning the giving of reading assignments as the results tend to be fruitless and futile.

A number of reasons can be offered to explain why the disadvantaged have little interest in reading. One reason may lie within the attitudes inherent in the family. Perhaps the atmosphere in the home is not conducive or reinforcing toward reading. The family may not be able to afford reading material or may not perceive practical value in reading, and consequently, cannot encourage it.

Another explanation may involve the disadvantaged student's limited experiential background which would limit his/her understandings of traditional classroom reading material; this limited understanding of reading in classes could create a negative reception toward reading. Closely related to this may be the lack of interesting and meaningful reading matter available to students in the school, and, too frequently, these students are bombarded by stories, articles, and textual material to which they can relate very little. In other words, the reading content is irrelevant, uninteresting, and un-identifiable to the background and experience of the students.

One final explanation concerns the act of reading as an information-getting process. Quite frequently, subject-area reading bears little practical value to the disadvantaged student's immediate or future life. They perceive the learning of dates, historical facts, mathematical problems without practical application, science theory involving little or no demonstrable utilization as not being meaningful, and hence, not worthy of reading.

Whether the above reasons occur alone or are multiple overlapping causes, the problem of interesting the disadvantaged in reading must be dealt with immediately. The task is not an easy one. Trying to overcome years of resistance and negativistic attitudes toward reading may seem insurmountable; however, if the secondary teacher views reading as important (and certainly most would), then the secondary teacher must assume the responsibility of motivating the disadvantaged.

The following techniques have been successful in motivating reading for the disadvantaged. Some techniques may be more successful than others, depending upon the atmosphere and psychological make-up of the classes. It is best, then, to keep an open, flexible, and experimental approach in mind toward using them; therefore, try as many as possible, if not all of them, during the course of the school year.

1. *Read yourself while students read*. As students read to themselves, they observe that the teacher, too, is reading; from their viewpoint, they are being reinforced that reading is valuable and important. In a subtle way, the teacher is stressing the value of reading to them.

2. *Read aloud to students*. This is rarely done. It is unfortunate that reading aloud to students is discontinued after elementary school. For some reason, it is considered an elementary practice exclusive to the early grades. Nothing could be further from the truth. Secondary students enjoy very much listening to interesting and enjoyable stories. By listening to these stories, student interest in reading similarly enjoyable stories on their own will increase. (This can effectively be accomplished through taping a story and replaying it for successive classes.)

3. *Set a paperback book on your desk*. Student observation again enters the situation. They become curious about the teacher's private reading interests. This, then, becomes an excellent opportunity for the teacher to share the paperback.

4. *Read aloud up to a climactic point and stop*. Assuming that all students have a common reading assignment to fulfill, the teacher can use this technique to capture their interest and motivation. Whether the teacher reads from the text itself or from a related text, the intention is to build up interest to an exciting point and stop. If the build-up has been exciting, the students will want to begin reading at the point where the teacher ended to find out what will happen next. Needless to say, this technique need not be restricted to narrative material; it may involve how to perform a task, how to operate a device, or how to improve a skill. The only requirement involved is that the teacher read something exciting.

5. *Dress-up or act-out reading material*. Allowing students to live the characters in a story or role-play historical figures in the history class will make the reading more concrete and meaningful. Students become more active participants as a result of their reading rather than passive recipients of that which they may not read at all.

6. *Establish a classroom library*. Departing occasionally from the traditional subject-area classroom materials can be beneficial toward motivating interest in reading. The disadvantaged student needs, as do all students, the opportunity to read those materials that personally interest him/her. Of course, teacher guidelines are necessary, but, through student contributions, a classroom library can be established in a corner of the room. Then class time should be given periodically to allow students to engage in their own freedom-of-choice reading.

7. *Advertise reading*. This technique needs to be reemphasized. Advertising can take the form of displaying posters, book jackets, and slogans of current magazines, books, and articles around the room. Students become sensitized toward reading. Their level of consciousness is raised as they are exposed to the visual stimulation of reading about the room. Books become a constant awareness—a reminder they cannot avoid.

8. *Utilize the newspaper as a medium for reading*. In terms of relevant reading material for the disadvantaged youth, the newspaper rates highly. Ranging from want-ads for getting a job, planning a budget, or furnishing a home to calculating live mathematical problems of playing the stock market, the newspaper provides an excellent resource for bringing the live and relevant world of the disadvantaged student into the classroom.

Motivating the disadvantaged is a difficult task; there are no easy answers when dealing with youth who come from complex backgrounds. A variety of techniques must be employed to determine which ones are successful. If the disadvantaged will not read, then they will learn very little. Motivating interest in reading is the initial step in achieving success toward learning through reading.

Motivating Farm Children to Read

by Mary June Roggenbuck

Why doesn't Davey, a bright second grader interested in what's happening in his world, enjoy reading? Davey has the ability to be one of the best readers in his class; instead he doesn't want to spend time with books. What's the explanation?

His reasons for lack of motivation and interest in contemporary reading textbooks have become a familiar refrain among special groups of children. Davey is a child who does not see himself or his family reflected either frequently or accurately in his reading texts. He lives on a large mechanized farm—living the kind of childhood he finds exciting, challenging, and intriguing. But the modern stories in his school readers emphasize an urban way of life, something he knows little of and cares less about.

Davey enjoys riding in trucks, helping with the cattle chores, watching machinery being repaired, participating in the harvesting of crops. As do many farm children, he spends a good deal of his out-of-school time with his family taking part in the agricultural activities on the family farms to the extent possible for a seven-year-old. Children in the stories of his reading series almost never do these things.

Like most farm children, this boy has a knowledge of his parents' work rarely found among children whose parents go away from home to work in factories or offices. As might be expected of a child who is growing up in the midst of his parents' work, Davey's vocabulary in the area of agriculture is highly technical. Yet reading-related activities at school have penalized him for his specialized knowledge and vocabulary. For instance, when asked to "name the animal"—a picture in his reading readiness book showed a black and white cow—he said the animal was a "Holstein," since he was acquainted with the breed of black and white cow in his family's herd. Although Davey's response was correct, the "right" answer demanded by the book was "cow." Thus, he was made to feel wrong.

Not only in vocabulary but also in content, Davey's reading material about farms is at odds with his own knowledge and experience. For example, a picture in his book featured a small brood of chicks mothered by a hen—a scene typical of a long-gone farming era. Even in his grand-parents' time, chicks were bought from hatcheries and kept warm by brooder stoves.

These examples suggest the confusion Davey faces when learning to read in his texts. Farm life as portrayed in his book does not correspond to life as he experiences it. Consequently, the text loses credibility, and Davey loses interest in reading.

The relationship between a child's interest and his or her success in learning to read is recognized by both publisher and educators. For exam-ple, the introduction to *Scott Foresman Reading Systems* stresses interest as "the cornerstone of success," while the *Lippincott Basic Reading Series* considers interest "a basic prerequisite to reading success."

Although publishers do strive to make reading interesting for children in our multifaceted society, the past has illustrated that the needs of minority groups tend to be overlooked in reading materials until a con-sciousness of the special needs of these children is raised. As American society becomes more and more urban, farm children such as Davey have become a minority in the nation's student population. Because of their environment, these children have special interests to which their reading materials should appeal.

Davey's lack of enthusiasm about the subject matter of his readers demonstrates that reading texts are not reaching farm children's interests which grow out of their involvement in agricultural activities.

DISTORTIONS

A further search for relevant stories about modern farm life led me to examine several series of reading texts known to be used in rural areas. These books were systematically examined for their portrayal of modern American farm life and people. Stories of contemporary ranch and reserva-tion life and that of migrant farm workers were excluded because the work-related activities or life-styles of the characters in them are different from those on large mechanized family farms.

In some of the series examined, children encounter the concept of "farmer" in their reading readiness books as a word to illustrate the sounds of the letter *f*, or on the primer level as a word to exemplify the suffix *-er*. In these instances, the pictured person we are expected to recognize as a farmer is as predictable as a policeman or a fireman: the farmer typically wears bibbed overalls and straw hat and holds a hand tool such as a fork, rake, or hoe—an inaccurate stereotyped image.

In workbook exercises in one series, these statements accompany illustrations of a stereotyped farmer: "The farmer has a feather" and "The fox is chasing the farmer.'' Although presented in this way to teach some aspect of reading, a farmer is shown in an inconsequential act and in a highly unlikely situation.

A farm boy or girl may well have seen foxes flee from farmers because s/he has seen the adults in his/her community hunt foxes to rid the area of these predators. To believe the reverse—a farmer being chased by a fox—would be incredible. Indeed, this child would instead be embarrassed seeing an adult like his/her father in the incongruous position of being chased by a fox. Instead of enhancing the self-image of the child, as instructional materials should do, such unrealistic portrayals lower the self-estimate of farm children regarding their people and their way of life.

In modern stories of these basal readers, farmers are sometimes called Farmer Small and Farmer Tom, an occupational label, instead of being identified as Mr. Small or Tom Smith. Once again farm children see an adult like their father treated less respectfully in books than in life. They have heard the banker or the attendant at the grain elevator address their father appropriately by name, never by ''Farmer.''

A CENTURY LATE

In these textbooks, hand tools are strongly linked to farmers, while tractors and other mechanized tools and equipment actually familiar to modern farm children are generally not in evidence. For example, in one manual the teacher is asked to have children identify the work a farmer might have done with the ''pieces of equipment'' shown, but there is nothing more sophisticated than a hand rake pictured. At least one series shows a farmer planting seeds manually. The farm child knows that while someone might plant flowers that way, a farmer certainly does not sow crops in this fashion.

One of the relatively few instances in which a farmer is associated with a tractor in a story situation appears in a workbook. The student is to conclude a story and the elicited conclusion is that the farmer's tractor is missing from the front of his/her hilltop house because it rolled down the hill while s/he was indoors eating. But the farm child knows tractors are costly equipment and that they are handled with care and safety precautions.

Some reading texts convey stereotypes of farmers and farm life not only in the farmer's appearance and activities but also in pictures of farm scenes. These tend to be idyllic—red hip-roofed barns with tall silos, rolling fields neatly fenced, occasionally small numbers of animals dotting the landscape. A farm child whose father has a pole barn, trench silos, and large numbers of livestock enclosed in a feedlot finds these scenes old-fashioned.

The damage done is not only to the farm child. Although stereotypes in illustrations are always harmful, they are especially so when they appear in textbooks in which the illustrations are an integral part of the instructional design. The teachers' manuals in these series again and again direct teachers to have children observe the pictures in the text and discuss them. Consequently, the stereotyped farmers, their outmoded activities, and romanticized farm scenes become deeply impressed upon all young readers unless a knowledgeable teacher or student counters them with up-to-date and accurate information.

In addition to contending with stereotypes presented in many of the texts, reading teachers are expected to supply information about farm life. For example, teachers are directed to have students compare and contrast aspects of city and country life as a suggested activity relative to stories on urban life. While the text presents some background for children to deal with urban life, the teachers themselves must provide the necessary re-sources for students to deal with the nonurban features of the activity. The teacher, however, may not have the background to do this.

In the instructions in some teachers' manuals, the teacher is directed to ask questions which will lead children to realize that modern farms might be different from those portrayed in the text. For exmple, in regard to a story about a scarecrow, the teacher should ask whether farmers still use scare-crows; in a story in which a boy milks a cow by hand, the teacher is to lead the children to deduce that this must be happening on a small farm because on large farms cows are milked by machine. Other directives to teachers would help to overcome stereotyping via illustrations: in an account of "The Barn," the teacher is to point out that not all barns are red.

COUNTER APPROACHES

In a few instances in the basal series examined, tractors are shown pulling wagons or other farm equipment; one illustration depicts cows being milked by machine; another illustrates a self-propelled combine harvester in action; the events of one story hinge upon the changing of oil in a farm truck.

However, until all publishers of basal readers become responsive to the need of modern farm children to see themselves, their families, and their way of life adequately reflected in reading texts, teachers must be especially selective in choosing a reading series so that it will help meet the special requirements of farm children. These teachers may need to look beyond basic reading texts, perhaps for trade books with stories on the child's reading level which provide an accurate and up-to-date picture of farm living.

Other media which portray farm life realistically might also be used. Generally teachers' manuals supply bibliographies of supplementary materials. However, these titles must also be evaluated in terms of the authenticity of their depiction of farm life. For recommended titles of newer materials, consult the school library media specialist.

Finally, teaching materials may need to be produced locally at the media center to supplement published instructional materials. The materials resulting from enrichment activities suggested in teachers' manuals, such as experience stories and picture files on modern farm life, could be added to the media center's resources for upcoming classes.

In summary, teachers must be sensitive to the needs of modern farm children to see themselves and their families reflected favorably and accurately in reading materials. Because these children's lives are so closely involved in the work-related activities of the family farm, they have acquired an extensive knowledge of agriculture and share in the family's pride and interest in their work. Unfortunately, instead of building upon this interest and pride to motivate farm children to read, some reading series tend to show farmers in unflattering and unrealistic ways. In any case, publishers' aims to interest farm children cannot be achieved so long as stereotypes exist in content and illustrations.

Until their reading materials have relevance and reality, Davey and other children like him will lack interest and incentive to read.

TEXTBOOK SERIES EXAMINED IN THE STUDY

Ginn Reading 360. Lexington, MA: Ginn and Co., 1973.
Holt Basic Reading System. New York: Holt, Rinehart and Winston, 1973.
Keys to Reading. Oklahoma City: The Economy Co., 1972.
Lippincott Basic Reading Series. Philadelphia: J.B. Lippincott Co., 1975.
Lippincott Reading Series. Philadelphia: J.B. Lippincott Co., 1975.
New Open Highways Program. Glenview, IL: Scott, Foresman and Co., 1974.
Read System. New York: American Book Co., 1971.
Scott Foresman Reading Systems. Glenview, IL: Scott, Foresman and Co., 1971.

Send-Home-Sheet

by Joseph M. Cronin

Dear Parent:

Television has become another member of your family and mine; we eat meals near it, learn from it, and spend more time with it than with any single individual. Television is central in our children's lives—as tutor, babysitter, teacher, entertainer, and salesperson, all rolled into one.

Has television grown so powerful we can no longer control it? No. But it very well might unless we act now to harness its influence and channel its awesome power. Television, like a potent drug, can either enhance or cripple a person's life. What can a parent do? Follow these guidelines—they *will* make a difference!

WHAT YOU CAN DO AT HOME

Start now. Many children are already habitual TV viewers by the age of two. Harmful viewing habits can be changed only by substituting new habits. Do a little at a time; *some* each day.

Put the TV in a little-used room. With the TV in an area away from the living room, family room, and other places where heavy family activity occurs, children will watch less and plan more what they want to watch.

Plan to have one night each week with the TV off. Meet as a family and pick a no-TV night. Decide whether you want to do things together or have "alone time."

Avoid using the TV as a babysitter. You would not leave your child alone in the care of a stranger. A television cannot respond to a cry for help, nor can it tell when a child is frightened.

Plan ahead what to watch. With *TV Guide* or TV supplement, decide what you and the kids will watch each night. Don't just turn on the set to see what's on.

Seek out programs made for kids. Help your children plan to watch programs designed for their ages, interests, and maturity.

Watch TV with your children. View their programs with them and help them evaluate what they're watching in light of your family's values and traditions.

Help kids distinguish between make-believe and real life on TV. Explain that the terror and violence on TV shows is acting and is not like real-life violence.

Discuss TV commercials selling junk food. Help young children see that ads are trying to persuade them to spend money by developing buying habits which could be unhealthy. Let your children help select nutritious family foods and snacks.

Use TV to start family activities. Make a list of TV-advertised products, and see how many you have in the house. Watch different news programs the same night, and see if all use the same lead stories. Play along with your favorite game show as a family or play your own version with the TV set off. Do a TV commercial product test and compare your results with theirs. Reinforce nonsexist programs by discussing them with your kids.

Find other leisure activities besides TV. Watching TV is relaxing, but so is a good crossword puzzle or game of cards. If you break the TV habit, your child will have a better chance of avoiding an addiction. Buy a puzzle book and work it together; a model rocket and help build it.

Read to your child. Start at an early age to help your child discover the magic in reading. Children of all ages enjoy being read to by their parents.

No need to try all these ideas at once. Start small by picking *one* you want to try and doing it. Post this list on your refrigerator and choose as a group one idea to try each week.

WHAT YOU AND SCHOOL CAN DO

Work with teacher and principal. Support use of quality educational TV programs in school.

Acknowledge that appropriate TV viewing is a skill that can be learned. Bring in speakers from PTA and local TV stations.

Let your feelings be known. Write newspapers, TV stations, networks, the FCC, and advertisers; tell them what you like and don't like.

———————

Teacher

Letter from England: Talking about Reading: Back to Basics?
Part I

by Aidan Chambers

As a young teacher just out of college twenty years ago I had the temerity to hang above my cupboard door—the book-stock cupboard being my only place of retreat—the legend: *You are here to practice the art of teaching, not to indulge in the science of education.* I am still healthily cautious about the findings of educational researchers. Frankly, I do not think there can be any such discipline as a "science" of education; and investigation of teaching-and-learning theory and practice is always done best by people who are teaching children regularly.

I mention this because it seems to me that a good deal of our present anxiety about the "problem" of literacy is as much a response to the results of spurious and wrong-headed educational research as it is a worry about the "problem" itself. I put quotation marks around that popular word *problem* because I do not believe there is a problem in any new sense. What we are noticing is that people—just to live their normal lives—now need greater skills as speakers, readers, and writers than they have ever needed before. Added to that, I think it is true to say that people are no longer prepared to accept for their children a minimum functional ability to read and write. We want more than that; in fact, I can see that in my lifetime the standards we expect from schools have steadily risen. And it happens, rightly, to be reading that presently concerns us.

Nevertheless, some things do worry me about the way we are, in many schools and homes, dealing with children as readers. Before coming to the crux of what I want to say, I would like to make a preliminary observation about one of my worries.

Consider this passage:

A biological schema, though elucidating certain aspects of the mastery of syntax, is of limited value in the study of the semantic and functional aspects of language acquisition. Skinner's notion of a single-factor reinforcement theory to account for the acquisition of complex language behavior is equally inadequate. The enormous impact of both of these approaches can be seen, perhaps, as a reaction to eclecticism, as a hunger for elegance of thought and "useful" theories. But language acquisition cannot be explained by a unitary statement of underlying processes. As Ervin-Tripp has stated in a recent review article (1966), "the basis of the child's most important and complex achievement (language) still remains unknown."[1]

I quote this here as a pretty modest example of the kind of jargonistic and tortured writing that flows from the pens of so many of the educationists who write about reading. It happens also to say something of quite startling importance, which happens also to be the truth. In plain English it says: *We do not know how children learn to speak and to read.*

Academics quite often have such important things to tell us. It seems to me that it is their responsibility—an obligation we pay them to exercise—to translate their ideas and findings into reasonably intelligent English which respects the mother tongue, the things they want to say, and the people to whom they wish to communicate.

For years now authorities have been trying to tell us that reading, and learning to read, is a mechanical process, something that can be analyzed, broken down into stages, and treated as a step-by-step operation, like making a car on a conveyor belt, bit being added to bit in a logical and planned sequence. And the authorities who have told us this have been wrong: "We do not know how children learn to read"; and we do not know very much about what happens when we read. Hence my healthy caution.

It would not have mattered what the authorities said if no one had listened. But all too many people have listened and have acted on what they have heard. So they threw out from their teaching—or lost them in their excitement for the latest academic fashion—some common-or-garden truths about reading and how people *teach themselves* to do it. We need to reassert these truths time and again and must not be afraid of the fact that their modesty requires no high flights of abstract jargon and that their appeal is slight to academics whose near-sinecure places depend upon "research findings" and skill in writing pseudo-scholarly discourse in language so oppressively ugly and esoteric that even people working in other sectors of the teaching profession find it not only tasteless but meaningless.

The first of these simple truths is that children become readers with the greatest ease and lasting effect when they are prepared for it, preferably from birth, by a daily experience of literature read aloud to them and an abundance of books shown to them. Speech comes first, words heard; reading follows. It is almost an axiom: You cannot begin to read what you have not heard said. Neglect of this preparatory relationship between child and language, child and book, means that by the age of five, a child is already in need of remedial teaching. The effect is just the same on the child's mental and imaginative growth as the lack of essential ingredient in his/her diet would be on his/her physical growth. Judged by this test, most children start school educationally undernourished; so most teaching in the early years is rehabilitative.

All along, the evidence for this has been under our noses. Instead of examining the successes and failures of children who were taught to read, we could have been learning essential lessons from children who became readers on their own without anybody teaching them.

One of our trustworthy academics in Britain, Margaret M. Clark, Reader in Educational Psychology at the University of Strathclyde in Scotland, did just that. I heartily commend to you her resulting book, *Young Fluent Readers*.[2] Dr. Clark studied 32 Glasgow children arriving at school, aged five, already able to read. They came, somewhat unexpectedly, from all sectors of the community, from the very well-off to the very poor. Among them, for instance, was the youngest child in a family of seven whose father was an unskilled manual worker. Only the youngest child had arrived at school able to read, but none of the others had had any difficulty learning. Throughout his last years in school the father had had a history of truancy, and he had left at fourteen; but he loved fairy stories and, Dr. Clark discovered, told them to his children. Both parents read for pleasure and information; went regularly to the public library, taking the children with them; and kept books in the home. No one had tried to teach the youngest child how to read; he had picked it up for himself.

Some of these things were true for every child in the group. All of them had been read to as a normal everyday event, and all of them had parents who read for themselves. The public library played an important part; "in catering for and in stimulating the interests of these children," it was a "striking feature of the study." And how far is learning to read a mechanically structured process? Margaret Clark says:

> The existence of children such as those in the present research must lead us to question to what extent and in what ways learning to read is a developmental process and whether there are essential sequential steps. It may be necessary to consider whether those steps which are frequently regarded as sequential are so only because of the structure within which we *teach* reading rather than the pattern within which children *learn* to read.[3]

One sure thing is done to most children starting school unable to read. They are drilled (there is no better word for it) through a reading series. Ironically, many of these series, combined with the way they are used by teachers, help create unwilling rather than willing readers. These materials turn reading into a boring chore. The reason is plain if one examines them not as colorfully illustrated, carefully graded teaching machines, but as literature. While preparing this article, I happened to be reading Bruno Bettelheim's over-abused book *The Uses of Enchantment* (Knopf). "The acquisition of skills," he writes, "including the ability to read, becomes devalued when what one has learned to read adds nothing of importance to one's life. . . . The idea that learning to read may enable one later to enrich one's life is experienced as an empty promise when the stories the child listens to, or is reading at the moment, are vacuous." Whatever one may think of Bettelheim's book in other respects, he states here nothing but the truth.

Many teachers imaginatively take pains to prepare their pupils for what used to be known in the trade as "reading readiness." Then, having raised their children's expectations high, they put before them the most bland, pointless, ill-written prose they can find. For this is the literary judgment one is forced to reach about the content of many reading series.

None of these, in fact, should or needs to fall below the standards of the best I Can Read stories, like *Frog and Toad Are Friends* (Harper). What looks, and is, linguistically simple in such books is also immediately and lastingly entertaining and possesses beneath the surface meaning of the text deeper meanings on which the imagination can dwell.

Reading series were born, I suppose, out of the same necessity that has led to computer-run teaching programs. Teachers have to teach far too many children at once, a situation getting worse, not better. In the Utopian circumstances of one teacher to three or four pupils, reading schemes would seem like weapons of torment to be left alone by civilized people. But faced with thirty or forty or more pupils—all, we have been led to think, needing to be *taught* to read by the teacher—the book-machines become essential.

Well, if we must go on using them, let us at least see to four protective defenses. First, children should be provided with the best possible series from the literary point of view. Second, they should be weaned onto proper books with all possible speed. Third, no one series or teaching method ought to be used, but a number of them should be offered which take into account the different ways people read—for example, those who "hear" the words as they read rather than "see" them (as I do) and those who, like my wife, "see" the words and do not "hear" them. And lastly, let us make sure that the reading series and the teaching done with them are part of an environment where the emphasis is on proper books and on having many of them always available to the children, whether they can read or not.

It does not seem at all surprising to me that in Britain *The Iron Giant: A Story in Five Nights* (Harper) by Ted Hughes is a far more successful book with children learning to read than any specially written text. How can you improve on the simplicity and potential for meaning and entertainment of a story that begins:

> The Iron Man came to the top of the cliff.
> How far had he walked? Nobody knows. Where had he come from?
> Nobody knows. How was he made? Nobody knows.
> Taller than a house, the Iron Man stood at the top of the cliff, on the very brink, in the darkness.

Nor does it seem odd to me that a boy of eight, slow in reading, insisted on leaving aside his supplementary reader in preference to *The Piemakers* (Lippincott) by Helen Cresswell, which he struggled through, word by carefully decoded word, from mid-October to late February, saying, when he at last finished it, that it was the best book he had ever had.

After all, we are not exactly lacking for books which—if they are not so superlatively fine as these—are certainly worth a child's attention and offer immediate as well as lasting rewards. Why, then, the woeful inadequacy of the book stocks in so many schools? The answer, I'm afraid, is that far too many teachers are depressingly ignorant about what is available.

Which brings me to my next point. Time and again we have it confirmed that the reading child depends upon the reading adult. To put it crudely, illiterates are made by illiterates. We cannot expect children to apply themselves with enthusiasm to the act of reading if they know that the adults around them have little enthusiasm for the activity. Teachers must be seen by children to read for their own enjoyment, not just for professional needs, and to talk about what they read, according books an important place in their lives.

The success we have in helping children become readers will depend not so much on our technical skills but upon the spirit we transmit of ourselves as readers. Next in importance comes the breadth and depth of our knowledge of the books we offer. Only out of such a ready catalog can we match child and book with the sort of spontaneous accuracy that is wanted time and again during a working day.

Even while acknowledging the importance of the adult, let us also recognize that children are pretty good at finding the right books for themselves. If they are given the chance. We should see that our job as teachers of reading is concerned with facilitating children in teaching themselves to read as much as it is with our teaching them to read. There should be daily opportunity for every child, no matter what his/her age, to browse through a collection of books.

There is, I am suggesting, a classic simplicity in the act of reading. First you select a book from many others. But selection is pointless unless you go on to read what you have chosen. Reading a text inevitably creates a response which expresses itself in various ways. Sometimes you want to rush off and tell a friend about what you've just read. Sometimes you are so strangely moved that to speak would be to destroy. Children, younger ones especially, often like to act out what they have read, re-creating it in their own image. And writers are not alone in being, essentially, readers who want to emulate the books they admire and find stimulating. But the most common response, the inevitable one in all true readers, is a resulting desire to read another book, one leading to another in a kind of excruciatingly pleasurable, unending chain reaction, a literary fission.

Selection: Reading: Response—leading to yet another selection. That is the literate reading circle. Once set in motion in our pupils, it becomes self-sustaining. This is what we should aim to achieve. But anyone whose work provides opportunity to look into many schools, as mine does, cannot help but lament how often that circle is never set turning because one part of it is neglected.

So full has the daily program in school become, with projects and integrated days in which pupils follow singly and in small groups their own instructional paths, that we all too often have allowed reading, as an activity in itself, to be squeezed out. Schools will often have rich stocks of literary books. They will often encourage their children to borrow from these stocks. But they do not provide time to read. Time to read, not in order to gather data or to find information to use in other work but in order to take pleasure in a text for its own sake. Time to read literature. We ought to insist that our schools provide time every day when everybody—adults and children—settles down and reads for no other purpose than to engage in that activity.

For the people who suffer most from the loss of reading time are the people who need it most, the children whose homes did not prepare them to be readers and do not encourage them to spend time reading out of school; homes without books and without the kind of atmosphere that helps children enjoy reading. For children in these circumstances—at least half of the children in most schools—*only* the school can provide the facilities and the time to read within secure and sympathetically disciplined surroundings.

What does Johnny need to become a reader? What are the basics we want to get back to? The answers stand out clearly. Children need to be surrounded by adults who are themselves literary readers possessing a ready knowledge of children's books. They need a large supply of books, wider in range than we often think is necessary, and daily self-directed browsing time in which to select the book for now. They need to hear everyday printed words read aloud and should be encouraged to respond to what they hear and to what they read for themselves. They need, more importantly than most other things, time to read, time in long enough periods to allow for absorbed attention and the pleasurable satisfaction that cannot come quickly, cannot be turned rapidly off and on, in the reading of a book. They should be helped to borrow books to take home and to buy books to keep. And we should examine far more urgently the links between home and school, between parents and teachers, so that both places help the child towards the same end.

Given all this, teachers and librarians could apply themselves with greater skill and vigor to the task that is theirs: how to lead children on from a superficial reading skill—decoding—to an appreciation of those books that yield the deepest meanings and the greatest pleasures. . . .

NOTES

1. Vera P. John, Vivian M. Horner, and Tomi D. Berney, "Story-telling: A Study of Sequential Speech in Young Children," in *Basic Studies on Reading*, eds. Harry Levin and Joanna P. Williams (New York: Basic Books, 1970).

2. Margaret M. Clark, *Young Fluent Readers* (Atlantic Highlands, NJ: Humanities Press, 1976).

3. Ibid.

PART
II

INTERESTS

Introduction

The discovery of a student's interests is an essential first step in the motivation process. Using this knowledge aids the teacher or librarian in selecting appropriate reading materials, which in turn stimulates a desire to read. The challenge for educators lies in discerning these interests and then developing and perhaps creating new ones. The articles in this section are representative of the many approaches which address this concern.

The first two articles deal with the importance and the nature of motivation. "Interests and Reading" by Sylvia M. Carter reviews studies on the relationship between interests and reading ability and habits. Her emphases on the historical setting and procedures for studying reading interests are useful in gaining a perspective of this complex issue. She concludes with suggestions for obtaining accurate information from students concerning their interests. Emmett Albert Betts challenges educators to "Capture Reading Motivation" based on the presupposition that motivation is innate in every learner and needs only to be cultivated. Betts regards interests as something to be "developed rather than unfolded." He offers illustrations with each key point and concludes that motivation is "the drive to learn which comes from within the learner and is both the cause and the effect of learning."

Observation of the student is the main idea in Betty S. Heathington's and J. Estill Alexander's article, "A Child-Based Observation Checklist to Assess Attitudes toward Reading." Rather than a one-time recording of stated attitudes and interests, their method is based on observable behavior over a period of time. They specify the suggested technique for use along with a ten-point checklist.

Several articles offer specific techniques for encouraging reading through special interests. Judith M. Barmore and Philip S. Morse support the need for interest centers in the classroom. In their article "Developing Lifelong Readers in the Middle Schools," they propose a variety of reading centers and give many examples. They also specify 21 types of reading materials and suggest a reading interest inventory to be completed by the student. Jack Cassidy, in his article on "Survival Reading," describes an approach to teaching basic skills through the use of learning centers. Individual and group activities are developed around the major topics of work, home, transportation, health/safety, recreation, and citizenship. He recommends that survival reading begin early rather than reserving it for high school instruction. Finally, Nicholas P. Criscuolo lists creative activities related to the natural interests students have for holidays and special occasions. Capitalizing on their excitement can enhance the reading program and increase motivation to read. Criscuolo also suggests books for further reading which highlight each special theme.

Interests and Reading

by Sylvia M. Carter

The topic of interests as related to reading is not a new one. Studies designed to investigate the relationship of pupil interests and reading are long-standing and numerous. The accumulated data presents the contemporary educational researcher with the opportunity to analyze a broad range of findings with a degree of historical perspective. However, it also poses for the analyst the problem of drawing generalizations from studies which often lack commonality of design, procedure, or terminology. This problem is amplified by the apparent impact of previous research. The historically early attempts to assess and to quantify general interests and reading interests appear to have influenced much of the subsequent research as well as the recommended procedures for teacher evaluation of pupil interests.

SELECTED RESEARCH ON GENERAL INTERESTS

Much of the research with children prior to the 1970s reported interests in terms of sex preferences. Findings reported boys and girls choosing what were then called sex-appropriate activities.[1] Tyler reported that differing interests were exhibited by boys and girls as early as age six and these sex associations of tasks he attributed to social role expectations.[2] Goodenough accounted for sex-typed differences with the suggestion that parents expected their children to exhibit differences in their interests varying with the sex of the child.[3] The research findings of Jersild and Tasch indicated that children's interests to a large degree were learned. These findings also indicated a decline in interests in things having to do with school as the children progressed in grade levels.[4]

The interests of the child are consistently described in the literature as unique, individual, but also environmentally and developmentally influenced.[5]

If indeed interests are to a degree learned, and if social role and parental expectations influence expressed interests, then certainly the studies of the period from 1930-1960 need to be replicated. Contemporary influences on social role expectations, on sex preferences for tasks, toys, activities, and perhaps books need to be examined for impact on [today's] students.

Over the past 25 years, research related to children's interests has often focused on interests as it relates to school activities: social studies interests,[6] health interests,[7] or art interests.[8] However, by far the largest number of research investigations of school related interests are devoted to reading activities.

READING INTERESTS OF PUPILS

The predominant categories for interpretation of reading interest research reflect the procedures in general interests research. The interpretation of the data places emphasis on the commonalities among groups (by age or grade, by intelligence, by achievement levels, by sex, by socioeconomic status, by cultural and ethnic labels) rather than the individuality of interests.

HISTORICAL PERSPECTIVE

Jordan described an 1897 study in Colorado as "the first extended study of children's interests in reading of the questionnaire type."[9] The study included 1500 pupils in grades 5 through high school levels. The subjects were asked among other things to indicate their preferences for "stories of adventure, of travel, of great men, of great women, love stories, ghost stories and war stories."[10] The pupils were to respond within this given range of answers.

This study by Bullock in 1897 raises the question of procedural and interpretative influence on subsequent research. The categories of reading interest as noted in this research are familiar ones and can be recognized in other early investigations as well as more recent ones.[11-15] These and similar categories have received criticism for their lack of specificity and the possibility of categorization of the same title in multiple categories.

By 1899 there had been some 25 studies that supported the conclusion that "early elementary students prefer literary (non-information) to non-literary presentations."[16]

It is common to find lists of generalizations concerning pupils' reading interests in teacher preparation and in-service texts. Such texts also generally caution the reader that interests fluctuate and are influenced by the individual's environment and experiences.[17-19] However, the categories of interests have remained very similar over almost 80 years of research. Many statements in current lists of generalizations are consistent with the results of the studies of the late 1800s.

PROCEDURES IN READING INTEREST RESEARCH

Direct observations and unobtrusive measures represent means of investigating pupil interest and have historical precedent.[20,21] Nonetheless, these methods are seldom discussed or recommended as interest assessment materials for classroom teachers. The oral and the written interview in questionnaire or inventory form have been among the most commonly recommended and used techniques in the history of interest research.

Research does not necessarily support this position. Shores and Carter found that students did not necessarily ask questions or express interests which reflected the stories or books that they said they wished to read.[22,23]

The individual interview has been described as an "oral question=naire." The crucial elements in this technique are the interviewer's skills, personableness and attention to procedural details. Some of the potential disadvantages of the interview involve: lack of training by the interviewer, interjection of interviewer bias, manipulation of large and varied numbers of responses,[24] and the time-consuming nature of the interview approach.[25] The individual interview gives the researcher the opportunity to follow up a subject's response with additional and extemporaneous questions if this appears appropriate.[26] The researcher and/or classroom teacher who uses this approach is expected to be aware of these limitations and opportunities.

These aspects of the interview technique are sometimes neglected in the interpretation of research and this may result in vague reporting of interview questions and procedures.

Many variations of these and other approaches are available and have been employed in contemporary reading interests research. Pupils have been asked to draw pictures that reflect their reading interests;[27] complete sentences to indicate their interests and preferences;[28] listen as a researcher or teacher reads aloud a set of story or poetry choices and then choose their preferred selections;[29-31] nonverbally select from a set of black and white pictures to indicate topics of interests;[32] select a picture preference based on visual components rather than actual illustrations of specific books;[33] select pictures presented on slides to indicate topics of interest;[34] participate in taped discussions of sharing periods;[35] or simply choose from among lists of reading selections or topics.[36]

The last of these approaches, the survey of story or book titles that pupils like and dislike, is a very often used procedure. Inferences are drawn from these forced choices about reading interests and the interests are subsequently categorized by literary form or pseudo-genre.

This procedure suffers from the criticism of limited scope and the demand of unrealistic response as does any forced choice task. A modification of this approach involves the construction of a forced choice task based on an individual's interview session. The interviewer draws a set of choices (selected perhaps according to the frequency and/or emphasis of responses) from subjects' expressed interests in the structured interview. The subject then ranks these personally expressed activities or materials according to preference.

SELECTED RESEARCH STUDIES ON READING INTERESTS

Elementary age pupils. A relatively large number of researchers have demonstrated that the primary age child as well as the pre-school child can indicate story or book preferences and interests when given age appropriate response options.[37-42]

These and other research findings through the early 1970s generally have enumerated primary age pupils' reading interests as: animals (realistic and fantasy), fairy tales, children (near and far away) and nature stories.[43-46]

More recent research findings indicate that first- and second-grade pupils may exhibit strong interest in realistic fiction and information categories as well.[47,48] Research findings from intermediate grade level children are generally described in terms of traditionally sex-oriented interests: that is, boys prefer stories of adventure, mystery, science and invention; girls choose "sentimental stories of home and school life, . . . romantic fiction."[49]

Investigations of reading interests indicate that children's interests change as they mature. Second-grade pupils as a group want to read about different topics or more nonliterary presentations than do first graders and so on throughout the progression of grade levels.[50-52] The developmental nature of these findings should not obscure the interpretation of the individual pupil's response to particular books and literary categories. Thousands of children in the elementary school were included in interest research by Norvell.[53] From this research, Norvell concluded support for disparity between pupil preferences and adult recommendations of children's books.

Adolescent and adult age groups. The 1940s and 1950s included significant research in reading interests of students of the secondary level as well as adults. However, the findings of these studies may have influenced some generalizations which were extended to younger subjects too. Strang reported a reading interests study involving subjects from 13-50 years of age.[54] Her findings emphasized individual differences rather than similarities. Norvell in his research with secondary students again criticized the tendency of adults to impose their standards, their likes and dislikes, on children and adolescents.[55] He hoped to make interest assessment more practical for the classroom teacher as well as to add research findings about secondary pupils' reading interests.[56]

Influence of sex differences. The preference by girls for traditionally labeled boy activity stories has been indicated in a number of studies from primary through secondary grade levels.[57-62] Some studies have concluded that achievement was improved when the vocabulary, illustrations, or text content were associated with the sex of the reader.[63-65]

Critics of literature for children and adolescents over the years have concluded after critical analysis that both male[66] and female[67] readers have had their interests neglected in both literature selections and tests.

Cultural, socioeconomic and ethnic influences. Cultural factors are considered important influences in children's preferences. Gibson and Levin assume a cause-and-effect relationship between American boys' lack of achievement in reading and the American lack of cultural valuing of reading for boys at this age level.[68] This assertion is supported with research by Johnson concerning cross-cultural preferences and achievement in reading.[69]

Leng, after reviewing a number of studies, concluded that indeed American girls expressed more desire to read than did American boys. However, he interpreted this finding as a possible indication that American boys may disclaim an expressed desire to read because of cultural values that label reading as a basically feminine pursuit.[70]

When Kirsch, Pehrsson, and Robinson looked at reading interests across ten countries, they found more similarities than differences in the 2,000 children from varying countries and cultures.[71] For example, the children in the first two years of school listed fairy tales and fantasies as their most preferred reading interests.

It has been generalized that age and sex are greater determiners of interests than are socioeconomic factors.[72] Liebler's research with inner-city high school students also supports this conclusion.[73] However, Wade reported reviewing research that suggested the child's socioeconomic status and environmental condition did significantly affect the choices and ranking of interest categories.[74] A number of studies have compared the interests of urban (inner city) children with those of suburban children. Zimet and Camp found their interests to be similar[75] while Johns and Ford and Koplyay found that inner-city children preferred to read about suburban rather than city themes.[76,77] Recent studies have investigated the effects of materials written and illustrated for Black pupils. Findings of many of these studies showed that Black pupils preferred illustrations depicting Black children but found the stories written in Black English or Black dialect to be more difficult than those written in standard English.[78-81]

Few studies are reported which relate to teacher skills and reading interests, children's literature, or subsequent teacher use of identified interests in relation to improving reading behaviors.[82-84] Cullinan pointed out that much of the available research criticized teacher training programs for lack of adequate or continuing preparation in children's literature for those who prepare to be elementary school teachers.[85]

Comments recommending teacher expertise with literature and interest assessment tools are prevalent. However, suggestions for implementing such recommendations are seldom offered.

IMPLICATIONS/SUGGESTIONS

A list of practical suggestions or recommendations concerning reading and interests must begin with teacher preparation programs. Pre-service and in-service programs for teachers must analyze the prerequisite skills necessary for administration and interpretation of reading interest measures. Appropriate adaptations in materials and procedures should be made in view of such an analysis.

In conjunction with this consideration, it would seem appropriate to increase the pre-service teacher's experience in reading and interpreting current research data as it supports or redirects traditional findings about reading interest.

Pre-service and in-service teachers also need increased encouragement and opportunity to work cooperatively with college and university faculty in research projects to investigate reading interests. The classroom practitioner and the researcher need one another's mutual expertise and support in research efforts.

The content relating to reading and pupil interests in pre-service reading education materials should be critically analyzed. The traditionally recommended procedures for the classroom teacher would be screened in light of contemporary research findings and implications.

Critical analysis of the term *interests* as related to reading needs to be made. The multiple entries as cited in reference sources as well as the contextual usages of the term should be examined. A part of the problem in interpreting research is the confusion and variance of definitions and contextual uses of the basic term *interests*.

Peer influence is often noted as a factor in pupil reading interests. Current research projects are investigating the use of sociograms in relating to pupil influence on the book interest of peers. That is, what happens to the book preferences of group members if the more popular children endorse or criticize specific book titles? Classroom practitioners at a broad range of grade levels need to look at such facets of reading interests and the effects of age/grade changes.

Learning centers are used in many of today's classrooms. Interest assessment centers based on the concept of learning centers present a potential observation plan for the teacher or researcher. Pupils could be observed and their interest behavior recorded in terms of questionnaires, checklists, case study reporting techniques or perhaps behavior or time analysis forms. This would allow the observer to record behaviors in structured settings as subjects moved from center to center. The composition of various centers could reflect procedures noted in previous research: (1) reading selections—selections from children's literature grouped according to variables such as readability, pseudo-genre, illustration categories, cultural content, character composition; (2) listening activities using tapes or records of selected stories; (3) drawing/art activities with pupil descriptions of story preferences; (4) standard questionnaires or inventories; (5) teacher- or researcher-directed activities allowing for individual interviewing; and (6) audiovisual center providing for pupil reaction to books before and after filmed versions of books and/or author interviews.

The procedure which asks children to draw a picture about what they would like to read or have read to them presents many research possibilities.[86] It offers the administration opportunity for individuals or groups. It also allows for the combination of informal interviewing, questioning, and recording of spontaneous pupil responses about their drawings and proposed stories. The teacher or researcher can ask clarifying questions or extend conversation in order to categorize pupil preferences in literary genre. This is also an efficient procedure timewise. Children can work individually on their drawings within a group setting. The teacher researcher can move from child to child to ask questions or take dictation about the drawing. This procedure may be repeated at regular intervals with the same children. The patterns of expressed interests may be analyzed.

The intensive individual interview is endorsed by Robinson and Weintraub. This is one of the most time-consuming procedures but also one of the most potentially productive. The interview procedure could form a part of the initial data for longitudinal research. Opinion and assumption currently dominate the literature concerning the stability and expression of reading interests over age, grade, and achievement changes. Longitudinal research is needed and research cooperatives within a school system could allow for multiple interviews and observations of individual subjects over an extended period of time.

This brief list represents not an intention to limit but one attempt to rethink some selected research findings. The review of reading interest research indicated that many opportunities exist, not only for drawing implications but for extending pragmatic and research activity.

NOTES

1. P. Boynton, "The Vocational Preferences of School Children," *Journal of Genetic Psychology* 49 (1936): 411-25.

2. Leona A. Tyler, "The Relationship of Interests to Abilities and Reputation among First-Grade Children," *Educational and Psychological Measurement* 11 (1951): 255-64.

3. Evelyn W. Goodenough, "Interest in Persons as an Aspect of Sex Difference in the Early Years," *Genetic Psychology Monograph* 55 (1957): 298-323.

4. Arthur Jersild and Ruth Tasch, *Children's Interests and What They*

Suggest for Education (New York: Columbia University, 1949).

5. Robert M. Goldenson, *The Encyclopedia of Human Behavior* (New York: Doubleday, 1970).

6. J.D. McAulay, "Social Studies Interest of the Primary-Grade Child," *Social Education* 26 (1962): 199-201.

7. Ruth Byler, Gertrude Lewis, and Ruth Totman, *Teach Us What We Want to Know* (New York: Mental Health Materials Center, Conn. State Board of Education, 1969).

8. Jane Brooks, "Familiar Antecedents and Adult Correlates of Artistic Interests in Childhood," *Journal of Personality* 41 (1973): 110-20.

9. Arthur Jordan, *Children's Interests in Reading* (New York: Columbia University, 1921).

10. Royal W. Bullock, "Some Observations on Children's Reading," *NEA Journal of Proceeding and Addresses* 36 (1897): 1015-21.

11. C. Wissler, "Interests of Children in Reading in the Elementary School," *Pedagogical Seminary* 5 (1899): 523-46.

12. C. Vostrovsky, "Children's Tasks in Reading," *Pedagogical Seminary* 6 (1899): 523-38.

13. Jordan, *Children's Interests in Reading*.

14. Alan Purves and Richard Beach, "Literature and the Reader: Research in Response to Literature, Reading Interests, and the Teaching of Literature," Final Report to the National Endowment for the Humanities, Project No. H69-0-129 (1972).

15. Helen Robinson and Samuel Weintraub, "Research Related to Children's Interests and to Developmental Values of Reading," *Library Trends* 22 (1973): 81-108.

16. Purves and Beach, "Literature and the Reader."

17. Helen Huus, "Interpreting Research in Children's Literature," in *Children, Books and Reading,* ed. Mildred Dawson (Newark, DE: International Reading Assoc., 1964), pp. 123-45.

18. Lawrence Hafner and Hayden Jolly, *Patterns of Teaching Reading in the Elementary School* (New York: Macmillan, 1972).

19. Albert Harris and Edward Sipay, *How to Increase Reading Ability,* 6th ed. (New York: David McKay, 1975).

20. M.B.C. True, "What My Pupils Read," *Education* 10 (1889): 42-45.

21. Joe Young West, *A Technique for Appraising Certain Observable Behavior of Children in Elementary Schools* (New York: Columbia University, 1937).

22. J. Harlan Shores, "Reading Interests and Information Needs of Children in Grades 4-8," *Elementary English* 31 (1954): 493-500; idem, "Reading Interest and Information Needs of High School Students," *Reading Teacher* 17 (1964): 536-44.

23. Sylvia M. Carter,"Interpreting Interests and Reading Interests of Pupils in Grades One through Three" (Ph.D. diss., University of Georgia, 1976).
24. Scarvia Anderson, Samuel Ball, and Richard Murphy, *Encyclopedia of Educational Evaluation* (San Francisco: Jossey-Bass, 1975).
25. Robinson and Weintraub, "Research Related to Children's Interests," pp. 81-108.
26. Anderson, Ball, and Murphy, *Encyclopedia of Educational Evaluation*.
27. Dorothy Kirsch, Robert Pehrsson, and H. Alan Robinson, "Expressed Reading Interests of Young Children: An International Study," in *New Horizons in Reading,* ed. John E. Merritt (Newark, DE: International Reading Assoc., 1976).
28. Thomas Boning and Richard Boning, "I'd Rather Read than . . .," *Reading Teacher* 10 (1957): 196-200.
29. Robert Emans, "What Do Children in the Inner City Like to Read?" *Elementary School Journal* 69 (1968): 118-22.
30. Richard C. Nelson, "Children's Poetry Preferences," *Elementary English* 43 (1966): 247-51.
31. Grace Pittman, "Young Children Enjoy Poetry," *Elementary English* 43 (1966): 56-59.
32. Robin Ford and Janos Koplyay, "Children's Story Preferences," *Reading Teacher* 22 (1968): 233-37.
33. John W. Stewig, "Children's Picture Preference," *Elementary English* 51 (1974): 1012-13.
34. Roberta Fairleigh, Linda Evard, and Ernest McDaniel, "A Picture Inventory to Measure Children's Reading Interests," *Elementary English* 51 (1974): 1011-12.
35. Loretta Byers, "Pupils' Interests and the Content of Primary Reading Texts," *Reading Teacher* 17 (1964): 227-33.
36. George Norvell, *What Boys and Girls Like to Read* (Morristown, NJ: Silver Burdett, 1958).
37. Paul Witty, Ann Coomer, and Dilla McBean, "Children's Choices of Favorite Books: A Study Conducted in Ten Elementary Schools," *Journal of Educational Psychology* 46 (1946): 266-78.
38. Helen Rogers and H. Alan Robinson, "Reading Interests of First Graders," *Elementary English* 40 (1963): 707-11.
39. Emans, "Children in the Inner City," pp. 118-22.
40. Ford and Koplyay, "Children's Story Preferences," pp. 233-37.
41. George Mason and William Blanton, "Story Content for Beginning Reading Instruction," *Elementary English* 48 (1971): 793-96.
42. Earl Rankin and Charlotte Thomas, "A Methodology for Studying Children's Reactions to Stories in First Grade Readers," *Reading Teacher* 22 (1968): 242-45, 299.

43. William S. Gray, "Physiology and Psychology of Reading," in *Encylopedia of Education,* 6th ed. (New York: Macmillan, 1960), pp. 1096-1114.

44. Witty, Coomer, and McBean, "Children's Choices of Favorite Books," pp. 266-78.

45. Loretta Byers, "Pupils' Interests and the Content of Primary Reading Texts.

46. John Wiberg and Marion Trost, "A Comparison between the Content of First Grade Primers and the Free Choice Library Selections Made by First Grade Students," *Elementary English* 47 (1970): 792-98.

47. Dorothy Kirsch, "From Athletes to Zebras—Young Children Want to Read about Them," *Elementary English* 52 (1975): 73-78.

48. Carter, "Interpreting Interests and Reading Interests of Pupils."

49. Albert Harris and Edward Sipay, *How to Increase Reading Ability,* 6th ed. (New York: David McKay, 1976).

50. Lewis M. Terman and Margaret Lima, *Children's Reading* (New York: Appleton, 1935).

51. Kirsch, "From Athletes to Zebras."

52. Kirsch, Pehrsson, and Robinson, "Reading Interests of Young Children."

53. Norvell, "Boys and Girls."

54. Ruth Strang, *Explorations in Reading Patterns* (Chicago: University of Chicago Press, 1942).

55. George Norvell, *The Reading Interests of Young People* (Boston: D.C. Heath, 1950).

56. George Norvell, *The Reading Interests of Young People* (East Lansing, MI: Michigan State University Press, 1973).

57. Cynthia Rose, Sara Zimet, and Gaston Blom, "Content Counts: Children Have Preferences in Reading Textbook Stories," *Elementary English* 49 (1972): 14-19.

58. Rogers and Robinson, "Reading Interests of First Graders," pp. 707-11.

59. Jo Stanchfield, "Boys Reading Interests as Revealed through Personal Conferences," *Reading Teacher* 16 (1962):41-44.

60. Wiberg and Trost, "First Grade Primers and Free Choice Library Selections," pp. 792-98.

61. Steven R. Asher, "Effect of Interest in Material on Sex Differences in Reading Comprehension," Final Report, Office of Research Grants (DHEW), Grant No. NE-G-00-30060 (1976).

62. Roberta Liebler, "Reading Interests of Black and Puerto Rican Inner-City High School Students," *Graduate Research in Education and Related Disciplines* (Spring-Summer 1973): 23-43.

63. Stanchfield, "Boys Reading Interests," pp. 41-44.

64. J. Schikedanz, *The Relationship of Sex-Typing of Reading to Reading Achievement and Reading Choice Behavior in Elementary School Boys* (Ann Arbor, MI: University Microfilms, 1975).

65. Asher, "Sex Differences in Reading Comprehension."

66. David Austin, Velma Clark, and Gladys Fichett, *Reading Rights for Boys* (New York: Appleton-Century-Crofts, Meredith, 1971).

67. I.L. Child, E. Potter, and E.M. Levine, "Children's Textbooks and Personality Development," *Psychological Monographs* 46 (1946): 60-63.

68. Eleanor Gibson and Harry Levin, *The Psychology of Reading* (Cambridge, MA: The MIT Press, 1975).

69. Dale Johnson, "Sex Differences in Reading across Cultures," *Reading Research Quarterly* 9 (1973): 67-86.

70. I.J. Leng, *Children in the Library* (Cardiff, U.K.: University of Wales Press, 1968).

71. Kirsch, Pehrsson, and Robinson, "Reading Interests of Young Children."

72. Harris and Sipay, "Increase Reading Ability."

73. Liebler, "Inner-City High School Students."

74. Elizabeth Wade, "Expressed Reading Preferences of Second-Grade Children in Selected Schools in Colorado," in *Reading Interests of Children and Young Adults,* ed. J.S. Kujoth (Metuchen, NJ: Scarecrow Press, 1970): 75-78.

75. Sara Zimet and Bonnie W. Camp, "A Comparison between the Content of Preferred School Library Book Selections Made by Inner-City and Suburban First Grade Students," *Elementary English* 51 (1974): 1004-06.

76. Jerry Johns, "Reading Preferences of Urban Students in Grades Four through Six," *Journal of Education* 68 (1975): 306-09.

77. Ford and Koplyay, "Children's Story Preferences," pp. 233-37.

78. R.V. Wiggins, *A Comparison of Children's Interest in and Attitude towards Reading Material Written in Standard and Black English Forms* (Ann Arbor, MI: University Microfilms, 1973).

79. G.C. Mathewson, "Children's Responses to Reading and Hearing Standard English and Non-Standard Dialect Stories: A Study of Evaluation and Comprehension" (Paper presented at the American Educational Research Association, New Orleans, Feburary 1973).

80. S.F. White, *A Study of the Relationship between Racial Illustrations Accompanying Stories in Basal Readers and Children's Preferences for Those Stories* (Ann Arbor, MI: University Microfilms, 1974).

81. G.W. Grant, *The Effect of Text Materials with Relevant Language, Illustrations and Content upon the Reading Achievement and Reading*

Preference (Attitude) of Black Primary and Intermediate Inner-City Students (Ann Arbor, MI: University Microfilms, 1974).

82. Samuel Weintraub et al., "IV-17 Reading Interests," *Reading Research Quarterly* 10 (1975): 427-34.

83. Albert J. Harris, "The Preparation of Classroom Teachers to Teach Reading," *Journal of Research and Development* 7 (1973): 11-18.

84. Purves and Beach, "Literature and the Reader."

85. Bernice Cullinan, "Teaching Literature to Children, 1966-1972," *Elementary English* 49 (1972): 1028-37.

86. Kirsch, Pehrsson, and Robinson, "Reading Interests of Young Children."

Capture Reading Motivation

by Emmett Albert Betts

What makes Sammy run? What causes Dick and Jane to explore reading treasures? Why does the new executive want to improve his reading behavior? Why do the gardener, the bookkeeper, the bird watcher, or other readers seek help in published materials? In short, what powerful motives result in positive action? These are the crucial questions—often overlooked in treatises on reading instruction—that merit consideration in depth.

These questions have caused psychologists and sociologists to produce thousands of researches and to write a spate of books, articles, and pamphlets under the rubric MOTIVATION. But motivation—a master key to learning—is not an ambiguous, fatuous concept. Instead motivation embraces knowing (cognitive factor) and emotions and feelings (affective factor) which put the learner in tune with books and other printed material. These cognitive and affective factors subtend a number of specifics (e.g., intent to learn, awareness of a personal need, knowledge of a topic) which are being expanded via research.

Motivation, which adds zest to learning, is only one facet of reading instruction—albeit, a master controller. The other two facets, word perception and comprehension, are dependent on motivation. Furthermore, effective reading instruction rests on one solid base—differentiation in terms of not only reading *levels* but also interests, needs (e.g., word perception and concepts), and cultures (e.g., home background).

This discussion deals with a fundamental factor in learning and teaching: motivation as readiness—with the WHY more than the how of learning. Motivation, word perception, and cognition (comprehension) are three *facets* of reading instruction—facets because they are aspects, not fragments of learning. But motivation is not viewed as one ambiguous, global concept; instead, nine factors from many are identified as crucial to the facilitation and escalation of pupil achievement in reading-study situations.

KNOWLEDGE

Doug was a serious-minded nine-year-old and an all-American boy who was becoming quite a competent authority on the War Between the States. He was often found in the deep study of articles in *American Heritage,* history books, and other sources of information. As he read more and more references, his *motivation* was captured by his increasing *knowledge*. In fact, he is now a major in history at a state university.

Knowledge, a cognitive factor in motivation, enlists the learner's efforts in many and diverse ways. The beginner, for example, may see only evergreen trees, but as s/he acquires more knowledge s/he learns to differentiate pines, spruce, fir, hemlock, and so on. The more the pupil learns about levels of abstraction (e.g., *horse-animal-life),* definite and indefinite terms (e.g., *ten-year-old Bill* vs. *young Bill),* shifts of meaning (e.g., metal *ball* to tennis *ball,* as shift of referent), and other semantic aspects of words, the more his/her interest in words is captured and expanded. The more a pupil learns about regularly spelled words (e.g., the spelling pattern *set-met-led-bed)* and irregularly spelled words (e.g., the sound /s/ represented by *(s)it, (c)ent, (sc)ent,* or the letter *s* representing different sounds in *(s)end, wa(s), (s)ure),* the more his/her interest is generated in phonics. Knowledge begets knowledge, but also begets motivation to learn.

SKILLS

Thirteen-year-old Charles in grade seven illustrates the fact that inadequate reading *skills* cause a learner to shun these activities. In our demonstration, Charles was completely frustrated with so-called preprimer words; the commonest words *the, is, to, and, said* were merely confusing black marks on the page. He had memorized the word *you* because it was "real odd" and he revealed some aptitude for learning "regularly" spelled words *can, sat, made, ride.* But he was confused by *said, was, come, here* and other irregularly common words. At the same time, Charles could comprehend and discuss intelligently a selection on the Sahara Desert when it was read to him. Hence, basic reading *skills* proved to be his undoing, and reading was an anathema to him.

When the pupils' skills are inadequate to cope with reading at certain levels of difficulty, they withdraw from the activity. On the other hand, when they have adequate skills for coping, they have attitudes of approaches and can become avid readers. Reading skills, therefore, are cognitive factors in motivation.

VALUES

Twelve-year-old Tony was a fugitive from learning with above-normal intelligence (on a WISC [Wechsler Intelligence Scale for Children], not a group test!) but only able to struggle in a preprimer which was far below his maturity in interests. Unfortunately, Tony was a prisoner of his father's attitude, who concluded our session with: "I don't see why Tony should learn to read. I can't read and I earn a good living for my family." In short, Tony's father placed zero *value* on the ability to read in this society, and Tony was faced with a cul-de-sac.

At age three, Marilyn could and did read widely. In fact, she could read any third grade reader with ease. Her father was a neurologist who read extensively; her mother was an avid reader. In Marilyn's home, reading was highly *valued,* although no special effort was made to teach her to read.

Many centuries ago, Plato stated the truism that what is honored in a community will be cultivated there. Corollary to the truism: when reading is honored in the home and community, children tend to acquire attitudes that lead to that behavior. In short, the impact of adult reading on pupil achievement is not to be underestimated by those charged with the responsibility for escalating reading instruction.

INTENT

When a beginner in reading knows the word *go* and cannot identify the word *Go,* s/he not only has a personal need to be satisfied but s/he has the *intent* to learn. After learning that *g* and *G* stand for the same sound and why the *G* was capitalized at the beginning of a sentence, his/her intent is satisfied and s/he is further motivated by his/her awareness of success.

INTENT to learn is a prepotent factor in the adult's drive to improve his/her ability to skim, to do rapid reading of light material, and to shift to study-type reading for technical material. Likewise, intent to learn is revealed by the beginner in reading who asks, "What is this word?" Furthermore, intention to remember what is read enhances retention— whether it is a telephone number or a fact about the speed of light. In short, intention to learn promotes higher motivation and, therefore, more attentive and less distractible activity.

To reinforce the learner's intention, teachers encourage (1) self-selection and categorizing of specific needs, (2) self-evaluation of what was learned. His/her intentions to learn are a built-in guarantee to keep on course until his/her goal is reached. They are self-actualizing—a prepriming for learning.

Intent is a WILL to learn terminated in satisfaction—an intrinsic reward.

AWARENESS OF SUCCESS

Jack, a twenty-year-old high-school graduate, sought after by a recruiter for a state university football team, was making rapid progress in his reading. But his reading disability was compounded by years of frustration in schools and consequently by a "dented" self-concept. For him, each directed reading-study activity was terminated by listing the down-to-earth specifics of "What I learned." But his *awareness of success* needed additional reinforcement; therefore, he was challenged to identify the titles of books: *Psychophysiology, Kinesis and Content, Cybernetics, Sociometry, Electroencephalography*. These and titles in other areas were read without hesitations, and the result usually elicited this comment, "I have learned more than I realized." Awareness of success fortified by the *learner's* verbalized *decision making* captures his spring of action and his perseverance to achieve his goals. The stronger the cognitive awareness of success is, the greater is the probability of a rise in the level of *aspiration*. (See *Aspiration* below.)

It is possible for a teacher or a parent to go through the ritual of a directed reading-study activity—using textbook, studybook, flash cards, and all the paraphernalia—without the child's awareness of what specifics are to be learned and without an awareness of "What I learned," if anything! When there is no intent to learn, there is no directional motivation. When there is no feedback to the learner regarding what s/he learned, the result is a meaningless, unproductive litany. To satisfy the learner's need for achievement-motivation, *intent* and *awareness of success* are wedded.

INTEREST

When a group from ages six to eighteen share their *interests* in a demonstration, they usually opt for reading about the real world. This *interest* may account for the fact that a book on *Dinosaurs* has long been a best seller. And it may be the reason why an "Informal Inventory of Interests" used the first day in a classroom or reading clinic reveals information *crucial* to the teacher's *understanding* of what spurs learners to read.

Interests are developed rather than unfolded. For cultural and other reasons, interests *tend* to be somewhat differentiated for boys and girls. At the same time boys are interested in biographies of *Portugee Phillips* and *Pilot Jack Knight,* girls may be turning to love stories. As the individual's internal environment changes and knowledge of the world is increased with "normal" development, interests tend to shift—from picture books and fairy tales to science, history, occupations, and fiction. And so, an ever-increasing range of dictionaries, encyclopedias, bulletins, and books is made accessible to developing and developed interests.

PERSONAL NEEDS

Amy, a twelve-year-old, was slow to catch on to hearing syllables in spoken words and seeing them in written words. During the demonstration of a directed reading-study activity, pupils were instructed to keep their own records of words on which they needed help—a new idea to them! Amy was encouraged when Charlotte, recognized by the group as a "good" reader, asked for help on *Neanderthal.* Help was given in a few seconds by writing the word on the board and underlining the first syllable *ne-.* This situation—two adjacent vowel letters in two different syllables, as in *giant, create,* and a spate of other words—was identified by both Amy and Charlotte as worth *follow-up.*

After the reading activity, each pupil quickly summarized word-perception needs and agreed to work with the teacher in small groups—one group of four to study syllabication. Amy proved to be a star learner on hearing the syllables in *running, after, thousand, pirate, radio, favorite, patriotic, dialogue.* Furthermore, she could identify the spelling of syllables. Using a rifle rather than a shotgun approach, the teacher aims at specific *needs* identified by the learners and, therefore, captures *motivation* to acquire a skill, the keystone to effective instruction.

Self-selection to meet a personal or felt need is a powerful concept in education, especially when it is expanded to include specificity in learning "What I need to know," and later "What I learned." The pupils may identify a group of words revealing word-perception *needs,* but the teacher helps them to classify, or categorize, those needs and to focus attention on the specifics, as *(qui)et-(pi)ano, m(oo)n-l(oo)k, (ou)t-c(ow).*

Likewise, the pupil, encouraged to ask for help on ideas s/he does not understand, is less likely to become a victim of verbalism when the teacher guides him/her into making the concept from his/her own personal experience. That is, s/he recognizes the fact that a teacher literally cannot give a concept or an attitude, that the learner must develop it from his/her own fund of knowledge. Self-selection requires decision making by both teacher and pupil in order to learn.

Awareness of a personal need (self-identified!)—an attitudinal factor—elicits *interest,* one starting point in learning word-perception skills and developing concepts. This need may be the study of a common spelling pattern (e.g., *cap-map-tap)* or a concept (e.g., time zones) following a directed reading-study activity. Or, this need may require the study of how the forty-niners panned for gold.

ASPIRATION

Jimmy, a twelve-year-old living near Cape [Kennedy], aspired to be an aeronautical engineer. In our demonstration, he identified in a flash *barometer, hypersonic,* and other multisyllable words gleaned from extensive reading in aeroscience. Jimmy is another living example of how *aspiration* influenced his *attitude* toward reading, activated positively his behavior, and reinforced values relevant to a truly innovative school culture which captures highly personal motivation to learn.

Aspiration is a goal—albeit a momentary goal—a learner sets for him/herself, which s/he expects to reach or has a strong desire to reach. Aspiration dictates to no small degree the level of future performance with attainable, appropriate tasks.

Success tends to raise the level of aspiration; failure, to lower the level and to result in eventual disillusionment. First, achievement of a goal may cause the learner to say, "Eureka. I did it!" Second, set up a desirable, *specific* goal (e.g., learning why a turtle's shell is arched or discovering the relation between spelling and pronunciation of *at, hat, bag, rag)* which is recognized as needed and attainable. Third, achievement of partial success (e.g., learning the syllables *sat, (sat)isfy, (Sat)urday)* toward a goal which is clearly understood leads to independence in word perception.

A learner's aspiration, or expectancy of achievement, is influenced by parents who "didn't like arithmetic so Johnny won't do well in the subject," who read and discuss what they read with the family, and who "expect Mary to bring home all A's on her report card." Aspiration, of course, is influenced by teachers who differentiate teaching in terms of learners' different skills, abilities, and motivations and who encourage the pupils to identify their own *specific* concept and word-perception needs.

ATTITUDES

James B., education editor for an international news agency, was confronted each morning by a desk piled high with news releases, articles, letters, and a spate of material demanding immediate attention. But he was a slow reader, with a vision problem requiring special vision training *before* attempting what he called "speed reading," and lacked versatility in shifting from skimming to rapid reading to critical and creative reading. Fortunately, he was well aware of a personal *need* and he had an *attitude* of approach—strong motivation for improving his abilities. But also he needed to learn *relaxation* via a "can-do" attitude for "shifting gears" in response to his purpose and systematic use of suggestion to achieve a satisfying state of composure. His improvement in ability to cope with his reading tasks was rapid and dramatic, with the *attitude* of approach reinforced by a combination of learnings.

George, age nine, stumbled over easy words, as *with* and *want*. A conference with the parents revealed that, during the preceding three years, the mother had "hit him on the head with a folded newspaper to get him to learn to spell these words." Now, George did not *see* these words on the printed page—the result of the mother's negative suggestion. He had developed a *negative attitude* that precluded learning the words.

Scott, age seven, was a victim of a principal's attitude. Although he could not read a preprimer, the principal insisted, over the parents' objections, that he be promoted to a regimented second grade where every child was given the same educational prescription—a second grade reader, a speller, and so on. His principal's rigid, unrealistic attitude produced a serious reading disability requiring the attention of a clinical psychologist as well as an understanding, special reading teacher.

There are *attitudes* that take a learner to reading, and there are attitudes that defeat the learner. These attitudes are *learned* in the home, in the school, and in activities with peers. As a consequence, learners are prisoners of attitudes that interfere with or facilitate their abilities to cope with reading-study situations.

MOTIVATION: EAGERNESS TO LEARN

Motivation—the drive to learn or the forces that activate reading to learn—comes from within the learner and is both a cause and effect of learning.

Knowledge + skills + values + intent + awareness of success = Interest

Information organized as knowledge, an awareness of relationships between ideas, generates interest; i.e., the more a pupil knows about a topic (e.g., birds or rocks) the greater is his/her interest in it.

Reading skills learned to the level of automation increase the probability of reading to learn.

The pupil's system of values (e.g., importance of reading) contributes intent to read to learn and vice versa.

Intention to learn and to remember is a self-actualizing factor.

Awareness of success via materials interesting and readable rewards the pupil's need for achievement. Achievement motivation is nurtured (reinforced) when the pupil is given immediate help on the application of learned skills and on the learning of new skills and when s/he is made aware of "What I learned."

Interest + personal needs + aspirations + attitudes = Motivation

In general, reading provides the pupil rewards and satisfactions to the degree that s/he is successful. Interests (preoccupations with self-selected reading activities) are learned.

A potent element in all learning is an awareness of a personal need, e.g., the need to identify the part of a word or to understand an idea in readable material.

Furthermore, self-selected, explicit purposes for reading tend to be more effective than teacher-dictated purposes.

Aspirations—future performance which a pupil hopes to reach—are raised by successful achievement of realistic goals.

Attitudes "of approach" to reading are nurtured via differentiated teaching and, thereby, contribute to motivation.

CONCLUSION

Motives, as antecedents to learning, have been discussed in terms of need-satisfying and goal-seeking behavior. Intrinsic motivation with its natural rewards has been emphasized rather than extrinsic motivation with its external rewards. Attention has been focused on getting wanted information and enjoyment in the belief that gold stars, play money, charts of books read, and other rewards are misleading—a snare and a delusion. Let dedicated teachers NOT ask how to motivate learners but how to capture their multiplicity of motivations.

A Child-Based Observation Checklist to Assess Attitudes toward Reading

by Betty S. Heathington
and J. Estill Alexander

Interest in the development and maintenance of positive attitudes toward reading is being voiced by classroom teachers, administrators, and reading specialists as they seek to make reading a process that children will use throughout their lives. Attitudes play an extremely vital role in establishing this lifelong habit.[1,2]

How does one assess children's feelings about reading? Several methods or instruments have been developed to aid teachers in this. Alexander and Filler have made a comprehensive study of these measurement devices and classified them according to type.[3] One type which is beneficial to classroom teachers is *observation.*

Observation has long been used by classroom teachers to determine weaknesses and strengths in reading skills. Miller advocates observation as the first tool that should be used.[4] Likewise, observation can also be useful in the affective realm, in diagnosing children's attitudes toward reading.

The value of observation lies in its comprehensiveness. Children's behaviors and comments can be viewed over a period of time and in many reading situations, providing the teacher with insight into how children feel about reading in various situations: school and nonschool reading activities, library reading, and general reading.

It is essential that significant behaviors to be observed be clearly outlined in advance. Random, extensive observation is not a luxury in which most teachers can engage. Unless they have a checklist of behaviors to look for, teachers may easily overlook the significant ones.

The authors examined the reading behaviors that would most accurately reflect children's attitudes toward reading. To obtain this information, children's views on the subject were probed—what behaviors do children think indicate positive and negative feelings toward reading?

CHILDREN COMMENT

The authors interviewed 60 children in grades one through six individually. They responded to two questions: What do children your age say and do when they dislike reading? What do they say and do when they like reading?

We categorized the comments according to reading environment: school, nonschool, library, and general.

The student with positive feelings or attitudes toward reading:

(School reading activities) feels happy when in reading group or reading circle; likes to read aloud to the class; feels happy reading at his/her desk; reads a lot of books in the classroom; goes to the bookshelf a lot; reads a lot in free time; raises her/his hand to read; brings books to school to read.

(Nonschool reading activities) likes to read to a parent; has lots of books at home; likes to read at bedtime; reads alone in his/her room at home; would rather read than watch TV; likes to read with friends after school; likes to read on trips; would rather read than play outside; likes to read outside.

(Library reading activities) likes to read in a library; likes to check out lots of books; goes to the library a lot; is always reading library books.

(General reading activities) reads all the time; feels happy when s/he reads; likes to read in a quiet place; talks about books s/he reads; enjoys reading.

The student with negative feelings or attitudes toward reading:

(School reading activities) would rather color than read; doesn't like to read aloud to the class; feels mad or sad when s/he goes to the reading circle; doesn't finish the stories that s/he starts; doesn't like to read in free time; just leaves books in his/her desk; doesn't like reading class; doesn't volunteer to read; is not on the right page or doesn't know the place when the group is reading together; thinks reading is hard work.

(Nonschool reading activities) doesn't have any books at home; would rather go to bed than read a book; would rather watch TV than read; would rather play after school.

(Library reading activities) never gets a book at the library; if asked to go to the library, says "no"; doesn't read her/his library books; is never seen taking home library books; doesn't go to the library; never gets around to reading the books s/he checks out.

(General reading activities) doesn't like to read; doesn't like books; doesn't like stories; looks sad; just looks at the pictures in a book; reads just a couple of pages and then quits; doesn't talk about reading; doesn't read; is never seen reading a book.

The comments supplied through these individual interviews were used to construct a quick assessment checklist (see figure) for teachers to use in observing children's attitudes toward reading. Certain behaviors were repeatedly mentioned: being happy while reading, desiring to read aloud, reading a lot of books, spending free time in reading, reading at home, choosing reading over other activities, desiring to go to the library, and talking about books which have been read.

The authors feel that a two-week period would be sufficient time to observe most of the situations that would be indicative of attitudes toward reading, i.e., the child has opportunity to read both in an organized and in a free time situation, to go to the library, to converse with the teacher, to finish a library book s/he checked out.

Checks in the "no" column alert the teacher to the child who may have a negative attitude in that particular area of reading activity. Further investigation can then be done and prescriptive activities designed to improve attitudes in that area.

OBSERVATION CHECKLIST TO ASSESS READING ATTITUDES

In the two-week period, has the child:	yes	no
1. Seemed happy when engaged in reading activities?	_____	_____
2. Volunteered to read aloud in class?	_____	_____
3. Read a book during free time?	_____	_____
4. Mentioned reading a book at home?	_____	_____
5. Chose reading over other activities (playing games, coloring, talking, etc.)?	_____	_____
6. Made requests to go to the library?	_____	_____
7. Checked out books at the library?	_____	_____
8. Talked about books s/he has read?	_____	_____
9. Finished most of the books s/he has started?	_____	_____
10. Mentioned books s/he has at home?	_____	_____

This assessment checklist is beneficial to the classroom teacher because: (1) it is a listing of behaviors children themselves feel are indicative of positive and negative attitudes toward reading; (2) it is concise and quick to use; (3) it can be used as a diagnostic tool for examining reading in various environments; (4) it is comprehensive in that it views reading behaviors over time and in many different situations.

NOTES

1. Thomas H. Estes, "A Scale to Measure Attitudes toward Reading," *Journal of Reading* 15 (1971): 135-38.
2. Charlotte S. Huck, "Strategies for Improving Interest and Appreciation

in Literature,'' in *Elementary School Language Arts,* eds. Paul C. Burns and Leo M. Schell (Chicago: Rand McNally, 1973), pp. 203-10.
3. J. Estill Alexander and Ronald Claude Filler, *Attitudes and Reading* (Newark, DE: International Reading Association, 1976).
4. Wilma H. Miller, *Reading Diagnosis Kit* (New York: Center for Applied Research in Education, 1974).

Developing Lifelong Readers in the Middle Schools

by Judith M. Barmore and Philip S. Morse

It is difficult to fault a curriculum goal which states as its priority the development of students who eventually become eager and enthusiastic lifelong readers. However, surveys by the National Opinion Research Center indicate that Americans read fewer books than citizens of many other countries including England, France, Germany, and the Scandinavian countries. Many adults in the United States have never read a book in its entirety. Approximately ten percent of the population read roughly eighty percent of the books. Many college graduates do not read one book a year, and many people cannot even think of a book they would like to read. Such facts suggest that we are not developing in our schools students who are enthusiastic, consistent readers as adults. Few if any children come to school with a negative attitude toward reading, but an uncomfortably large number of students do not like to read by the time they reach middle level schools. The numbers are proportionately higher by the time a student has graduated from high school.

Many children in elementary school experience early failure because they do not read at the grade norm defined for their chronological age. Students feel they cannot read so they begin to dislike reading. Aversion leads to avoidance and skill development slows down or ceases. Even many students who read reasonably well do so only for the grades they anticipate they will receive or for the approval of their teachers or parents. Once they are on their own the central motivation for reading often disappears. Such students become the American adults who feel that reading is a chore rather than a source of pleasure or a vehicle for learning for the rest of one's life.

Many of our practices in the teaching of reading and literature in the middle school only build and reinforce negative attitudes toward reading. Whether heterogeneously or homogeneously grouped, the middle level classroom will include students who have a variety of needs and interests that cannot be met in a situation where the entire class works simultaneously on common teacher-assigned materials. As teachers we sometimes assign materials that are geared too high for many students and thus reduce the process of reading to one of painful memorization. When students fail to meet our expectations, we are inclined to assign workbook pages, skill builders, or other activities that only tend to reinforce the feeling that reading is an unpleasant chore. Even when we attempt to individualize, we often minimize the role of student choice by requiring the reading of a certain number of pages, answering questions about the reading, or completing additional skill-related exercises. The student's personal feelings and reactions are often overlooked, and there is little opportunity for interaction between students concerning the materials they have read. The value of literature does not lie in its inherent content but in what it can do for the student personally. If we as teachers really want our students to become lifelong readers and learners, we must work with pupils in constructing a program they find creative and appealing. We must provide an attractive, open, supportive environment that will stimulate and build a general interest in reading.

Of central importance is creating an atmosphere where a student feels comfortable, safe, and able to share his/her reading interests, reactions, and insights with the teacher and other students. A feeling of security within the classroom will enable a student to feel that his/her own response, even though it may be subjective and idiosyncratic, will be taken seriously and respected. A student will begin to enjoy literature and reading more when s/he feels the validity of his/her spontaneous and honest experience.

In "A Scale to Measure Attitudes toward Reading" Thomas H. Estes states, "How students feel about reading is as important as whether they are able to read, for, as is true for most abilities, the value of reading ability lies in its use rather than its possession."[1] Estes has constructed an attitude scale appropriate for middle school use and which is uncomplicated to administer and score. Estes claims that by using the scale as a pre- and post-test the teacher can note attitude changes toward reading during the school year. A student should know the importance of a positive attitude toward reading and the teacher should help the middle schooler become aware of his/her feelings toward reading and why s/he feels that way.

The teacher himself/herself should possess an active and lively interest in books. S/He should talk about and bring in books s/he is reading and share interesting articles, stories, and jokes from newspapers, magazines, and other sources with the class. Students should be encouraged to do the same. When the school or public library purchases new books or other materials, the librarian or teacher should discuss them with the students. During free reading time everyone should read, including the teacher. Oral reading should not end in the elementary school. All age levels can enjoy and benefit from well-read and interesting selections.

As a beginning step, the physical area of the middle school classroom can be structured to provide room for reading interest centers. An interest center is a space arranged in such a way that learning can occur without the teacher's constant, direct influence. Reading centers also enable the teacher to devote more attention to individuals and small groups of students. If space is limited, activities and materials for the centers can be displayed on the sides of file cabinets, on the back of bookcases, or on a piece of cloth hanging from a dowel. Room dividers also make good display areas.

Some reading centers that may interest middle schoolers include the following:

1. *Sports Corner*—Books, magazines, short stories, filmstrips, athletic programs, baseball, football or hockey cards, charts of sports teams and their current rankings, and scrapbooks of local teams' game results are a few items that can be displayed. Activity cards might include the categorization of players by team or batting average, putting together an all-star team, contributing to a scrapbook (a stimulus to newspaper reading), keeping up statistics charts, and finding information about certain players.

2. *Hobby Center*—Have the students bring in hobbies and any reading material pertaining to their hobby. Students can describe their hobbies, what they like about them, and why they think others might enjoy them.

3. *A "Kids Did It" Corner*—Students can bring in projects they make or display awards or accomplishments. If a student has won a blue ribbon showing his/her horse or dog, s/he could bring in his/her ribbon and write about his/her experience. Such descriptions could be in a special folder or on display for other students to read. Others might tell about a project they completed in another class or in an outside school organization such as Scouts or 4-H.

4. *Catalog Center*—Sears', Penney's, and stamp, gun, coin or other catalogs can be displayed. Again, activity cards can be made to accompany them. Sample activities might include spending a given amount of money on sports gear/clothes, comparing prices and features of given products, and writing advertisements about products.

5. *Center for Writing Books*—Having students write their own books is an especially good project for poor readers. However, all students will gain from such an activity. Students can write books for primary children in the district and if possible they can read the books to younger students. One advantage is that a poor middle school reader will not feel inadequate using a simple vocabulary. His/her self-esteem and pride will also be boosted when s/he sees the enjoyment a younger student derives from his/her product. The books can be bound by covering pieces of cardboard with

cloth or contact paper for a cover. If an old typewriter is available, students can even type up the pages of the book. Middle school and junior high school students can also draw their own illustrations or cut them from old books or magazines.

6. *Listening and Viewing Corner*—Individual filmstrip viewers with tape players and/or record players and earphones can be provided. Students can listen to recordings while following along in their books.

7. *Everyday Materials Center*—Display a telephone book, *T.V. Guide,* or brochures on automobiles, motorcycles, or snowmobiles. Task cards can be constructed for each type of material. For instance, one assignment emphasizing dictionary skills asks students to locate certain telephone numbers. Middle level students can also use the yellow pages to identify a place where they can purchase a special item or perhaps find the number of a doctor or dentist.

Another task states an everyday problem: "Your new Honda minibike just blew a tire. Where could you call to get it repaired?" For an assignment the student might even telephone some of the places for information.

T.V. Guide can be used in several ways. Students can read the section "Movies for the Week," select a movie, tell why they selected it and record the channel, day, and time it is showing. Students can classify television shows and tabulate whether there are more crime or comedy presentations aired in a week's time.

READING MATERIALS IN THE MIDDLE SCHOOL

Because students at the middle school level are becoming increasingly aware of the outside world, it is important to offer a variety of materials that reflect the wide range of interests and abilities. Because some students at this age level have little or no motivation to read, the material must be interesting, pertinent, and stimulating, and the ability level should span at least six reading levels.

Newspapers, magazines, and paperback books are three obvious sources which import the outside world into the classroom. Other non-standard reading materials that can be used in the classroom include:

1. *Greeting Cards*—Middle schoolers love to read contemporary cards. They can also be challenged to write their own.

2. *Comic Strips*—These can be used in many ways. Cut sections apart and challenge students to sequence the story. Cover the dialog and ask the students to write their own. Some students may even want to draw their own comics with appropriate dialog.

3. *Sheet Music*—Reading and studying the lyrics of a song can be an effective way to introduce poetry. Students can even write their own lyrics to songs they like.

4. *Record Jackets*—Many record jackets offer information about the artist in the form of a short biographical sketch. This can spark a beginning interest in biographies for a student.

5. *Automobile, Minibike, Motorcyle, Snowmobile Parts Catalogs and Repair Manuals*—Many kids enjoy reading about these topics and can apply study skills in locating various parts.

6. *"How To" Manuals*—Free manuals on macramé, knitting, plants and many other subjects can be readily obtained.

7. *Posters*—Posters are excellent starters for discussion or creative writing since many of them have sayings or poems that can be read for pleasure or as part of an assignment. Posters come free in many magazines, including *Teacher, Instructor, World,* and *Learning.*

8. *Souvenir Pamphlets*—Students and teachers can bring these in after they have attended a concert, sports event or other happening. They can tell the class about it and encourage others to read articles or other interesting tidbits in the booklet.

9. *Advertising Circulars for Cars, Motorcycles, Snowmobiles, and Sporting Goods*—Students can choose an item they would like to purchase and list safety features or other reasons why they might choose that particular product.

10. *Miscellaneous Pamphlets*—There are literally hundreds of these that students might be interested in. Some examples include backpacking guides, wilderness survival, first aid, horse care, pet care, and wild plant and animal identification. The United States Government Printing Office is an excellent source for inexpensive and free books and pamphlets on a variety of subjects. The home extension office in local counties also offers an abundance of free pamphlets and other materials.

11. *Advertisements for Record, Tape, and Book Clubs*—Students can read and describe how they might join. They can also choose an order and write it up.

12. *Driver's Manual*—There are few middle school and junior high school students who are not interested in learning how to drive. Manuals can be studied and discussed and a sample test can be introduced for practice. Students might also make up their own tests (good for clarity and coherence in writing).

13. *Snowmobile and Boat Operators' Guides*—Students can discuss or write down fair criteria for being allowed to operate the vehicles.

14. *Pins, Buttons, and Bumper Stickers*—Students love any new mod buttons. They can discuss the meaning of many of the sayings, how clever they are, and even try composing their own. All such efforts should be displayed.

15. *Game Instructions and Directions for Assembling Items*—Have students read some and see if other members of the class can follow the

directions by using actual games or objects to be assembled. (A new, unassembled bicycle is a good challenge. It also saves *you* hours of wear and tear!)

16. *Travel Brochures*—Have a student plan a trip, research the country or countries, and decide on his/her itinerary.

17. *Placemats*—Have students begin collecting these at restaurants. Many of them have interesting tidbits of information that can be read or used as the basis for further research on a particular subject.

18. *Jokebooks or Collections of Students' Jokes*—It is fun to share jokes whether they be from books in class or from outside sources students bring in (it might be a good idea to "hear" some of these jokes before public consumption!). Jokes are also an effective study of story sequence and descriptive, pithy language. Students can also write their own jokes.

19. *Paperback Catalogs*—The class can even place orders for the classroom or school library.

20. *Photograph Albums*—Have students bring in their favorite home pictures and let them describe their significance or meaning to the class or write about them. Display them so that students can read each other's stories and descriptions.

21. *Road Maps*—Take turns finding towns or the distance from one point to another. Have students bring in maps of the area around which they were born or go on vacation. Again, students can write about their favorite spot and their papers can be displayed and read by members of the class.

OTHER TECHNIQUES FOR THE PROMOTION OF READING IN THE MIDDLE SCHOOL

Open and free discussion of books is another important way to create interest and enthusiasm for reading among middle school students. In *Explorations in the Teaching of Secondary English,* Stephen Judy asserts that "nothing will help to reinforce students' reading habits as quickly as being able to talk with the teacher, freely and openly, about some of the interesting things that happen in books."[2] Students often enjoy simply talking about a book spontaneously with friends.

The teacher should be a contributor to these discussions. S/He need not feel that his/her role is always one of improving the students tastes or in helping them find the correct meaning to a reading selection. A rudimentary response on an emotional level is the first step in getting a student to go deeper into a work. Unless the teacher is willing to accept honestly a student's initial response, no matter how idiosyncratic or personal, there is little chance of getting the student to evaluate the work at subsequently higher levels of meaning and sophistication.

Another way to assess accurately the reading interests of students and to determine the kinds of materials and activities they need is to administer a Reading Interest Inventory. (See sample on page 82.)

Still other ways of promoting an interest in reading include the displaying of books so that the entire cover, rather than just the spine, shows. An inexpensive simple book rack for such a purpose can be made with a piece of pegboard and hooks. Bulletin boards should attractively display reading materials, and students should be allowed to participate in their construction. Students' work and the items they bring in should be constantly displayed, including books and materials related to what they are reading. The teacher can promote book club sales and hold simulated book auctions where the books bought could be used for assigned work. The teacher could provide interesting bits of information about various authors and the class could correspond with writers. The class can participate in periodic book reviews and make frequent trips to the library.

Games can also be used to stimulate an interest in reading. One example is a take-off on "To Tell the Truth." One student who reads a book and two imposters who pretend to have read it answer questions from classmates about the book. The reader of the book must answer truthfully. The class votes on the student they think is telling the truth, after which the real reader stands up.

We are not tinkering with bits and pieces of the curriculum in suggesting that we must change some of the structure and even the approach to the teaching of reading in the middle school. However, if we can create a healthy, positive, psychological environment within the framework of an attractive and stimulating physical setting, we feel that the chances for promoting students who feel good about reading and who will continue to read for the rest of their lives should increase considerably, if not dramatically.

NOTES

1. Thomas H. Estes, "A Scale to Measure Attitudes toward Reading," *Journal of Reading* 15 (November 1971): 135-38.
2. Stephen N. Judy, *Explorations in the Teaching of Secondary English: A Source Book for Experimental Teaching* (New York: Dodd, Mead, 1975), p. 134.

SAMPLE READING INTEREST INVENTORY

My Interest in Reading

1. What are your special interests or hobbies outside of school? __
   _____

2. How do you feel about reading? Are there any special reasons you feel this way? _____

3. What is your favorite type of reading? (short stories, stories about sports, mystery stories, adventure stories, poems, etc.) _____

4. Do you read a daily newspaper? If so, what sections do you like best? _____

5. Do you read any magazines? What are they? _____
   _____

6. Do you like to read comic books? What are some of your favorites? _____
   _____

7. If you have read a book recently, write down the title of that book. If you liked it, tell me why. If you did not like it, tell me why. _____
   _____

8. Do you like to have your teacher read to you? If so, is there anything special you would like to hear? _____
   _____

9. Do you like to read in regular reading books? Why or why not?
   _____

10. Do you like to do book reports? If so, what kind (written, oral, in a group, alone with the teacher)? If not, how else could you let your teacher know that you really read the book? _____
   _____
   _____

11. Do you like to use the school library? Why or why not? _____
   _____

12. Do you like to use a public library? If so, which one? If not, why not? _____
   _____

13. Is it easy for you to find books in the library? _____
14. Do you like to use the card catalog? _____
    Do you feel that you understand how to use it? _____
15. Do you like to use reference materials? _____

My Interest in Reading, cont'd.

16. Which reference materials have you used?
    a. Dictionary ___
    b. Encyclopedia ___
    c. Atlas ___
    d. World Almanac ___
    e. *Book Review Digest* ___
    f. Biographical Dictionaries *(Who's Who in America, Who Was Who in America, Current Biography, etc.)* ___
    g. *Reader's Guide to Periodical Literature* ___
    h. *Roget's Thesaurus* ___
    i. Other ___
17. How do you feel about reading your social studies book? ___

18. Do you find word problems in math difficult to do? Why? ___

Survival Reading

by Jack Cassidy

"U.S. Illiteracy Rate: Nearly 1 of 5 Adults." Headlines like this one from a recent Chicago newspaper have focused attention on illiteracy in the United States. Most of the people referred to as illiterates today are functional illiterates. They have some reading and writing skills but are not capable of performing some of the basic tasks required to survive in our modern society. For example, they cannot read recipes, complicated signs, or job applications.

State departments of education, legislatures, and school districts have responded to this dilemma by calling for an increased emphasis in the schools on these so-called survival skills. Unfortunately, almost all of the attention has been given at the high school level.

The Newark School District in Delaware has sought to make sure that some of these survival skills are also taught at the elementary and middle school levels. As part of our Project CARE (Content Area Reading Enrichment), teachers develop survival kits that can be utilized in a variety of ways in individual classrooms. One of the most effective techniques we've found for introducing survival skills for younger students is through learning centers. [See *Teacher*, January 1977, pp. 50 and 70 for more on Project CARE.]

Each kit contains approximately 30 independent individual activities and five group activities. The activities are based on survival materials drawn from six general areas: work, home, health and safety, transportation, recreation, and citizenship. Many times the decision to put a particular activity in one category rather than another is purely arbitrary. The grade levels the activities were designed for are given, but most could cover several grade levels or be adapted. The one example described for each area will give you an idea of the direction to take for many other activities. Remember, in all survival materials it's important to concentrate on those skills most important for comprehending the given material.

1. WORK

Correctly filling out application forms is a very important task in adult life. One second-grade teacher developed an "Application Station" to give her six- and seven-year-olds some early practice. Each week half the class spent time at the station filling out forms like the one shown here. Because it describes actual school tasks, it makes a meaningful parallel to the adult working world.

Many of the responses to questions two and three are very interesting. In response to the question, "Why should I hire you for the job?" one second grader answered, "Because you like me." His teacher gave him the job.

Name: _____

Address: _____

1. Check the job you are applying for.

    ___ watering the plants   ___ cleaning the fish tank

    ___ leading the line   ___ cleaning the sink

    ___ sweeping the floor   ___ washing the boards

    ___ clapping board erasers   ___ collecting lunch money

2. Why are you applying for this job?

3. Why should I hire you for this job?

4. If you can't have this job, what other job would you like?

---

2. HOME

Telephone books, recipes, package labels, appliance directions and advertisements all play a part in children's as well as adults' lives. They also provide excellent sources for teaching survival reading.

One sixth-grade teacher developed a whole series of independent folder stations based on recipes. Each manila folder has a recipe pasted on the left side. On the right side, there are a series of activities designed to build vocabulary knowledge or basic comprehension. There was purposely no attempt to rewrite the recipes at a lower level. Below are a typical recipe and activities focusing on two skills crucial for following recipes—vocabulary and recognizing correct sequence.

BOSTON BAKED BEANS

Six cups dried pea or navy beans
One pound salt pork
1½ tablespoons dry mustard
1¼ tablespoons salt
1 teaspoon pepper
1¼ cups molasses
3 medium onions quartered

Rinse beans, cover with water, and soak overnight. Drain beans. Place in kettle with enough water to cover. Add onions. Bring to boil, then reduce to simmer for 45 minutes, or until beans are just tender, adding enough boiling water to cover as needed. Drain. Simmer salt pork in water to cover for ten minutes. Slice off two thin strips; place one at bottom of bean casserole or baking pan (15½ x 10½ in.); dice the other and set aside; score the rind of the remaining piece. Mix mustard and remaining ingredients until thoroughly blended. In casserole, alternately layer the beans, molasses mixture and diced pork until all are used up. Place salt pork into center of beans leaving only rind exposed. Add enough boiling water to cover beans. Cover tightly; place in very slow oven (250 F.) for eight hours, adding only enough boiling water as needed to cover beans. Uncover, during last hour of baking, allowing rind to become crisp. Do not add any water during last 90 minutes of cooking. Serves ten.

ACTIVITIES

1. Vocabulary: Define the following words as they are used in this recipe.

simmer	*ingredients*
casserole	*kettle*
dice	*salt pork*
score	*quartered*
rind	*layer*

2. Comprehension: Put the following steps in the recipe in the right order.

A. Simmer salt pork.
B. Cook for eight hours.
C. Soak beans overnight.
D. Mix in mustard.
E. Layer the beans, molasses, and pork.
F. Put the salt pork in the middle of the beans.
G. Bring beans to a boil then simmer.
H. Slice thin strips of pork.
I. Do not add water for the last 90 minutes.
J. Add onions.

3. TRANSPORTATION

In our highly mobile society, it is very important that students be able to read road signs, train schedules, and road maps. "Road to Survival," a small-group activity game, was developed by two fourth-grade teachers. The game board, which has 27 spaces from "start" to "stop" (drawn to look like a real stop sign), is pasted on the inside of a manila folder for easy storage.

The only other materials needed are word cards (with words or phrases on one side and their definitions on the other), a die, and several buttons.

The words and phrases our teachers put on the cards are: *beware of crosswinds, caution, detour, emergency vehicles only, freeway, junction 104, loading zone, m.p.h., merge left (right), no "U" turns, put on chains, R.R., resume speed, slide area, speed checked by radar, steep grade, stop for pedestrians, truck route, military reservation, watch for flagmen, prohibited,* and *toll ahead.*

"Road to Survival" directions are:

1. Each player should choose one button.
2. Place your button at the starting line.
3. Roll the die. Draw the top card from the word pile. Read the word or phrase and define the underlined word. (Check your definition by looking on the back of the card.)
4. If your definition is correct, move the number of spaces on the die.
5. The first person finished wins.

"Road to Survival" can be easily modified by changing the word cards. It can be further simplified by having the children merely pronounce the words rather than define them.

4. HEALTH/SAFETY

Reading items related to a person's health and safety are undeniably survival reading materials. In some instances, it is vital that even first graders be able to read materials relevant to their health or safety. One first-grade teacher developed "Medicentration," a variation of the game "Concentration," to reinforce the ability to recognize words and phrases often found on medicine labels. She and her students had already discussed their meaning and importance before they played the game. She wrote the following 17 terms on two sets of index cards: *caution; tablet; warning; laxative; don't use in, near, around eyes or face; not for external use; not for internal use; external use only; antidote; poison; poisonous; keep out of reach of children; tablespoon; teaspoon; drops; nostril; adult dosage.* It's best not to use felt-tip pens on the cards because the color usually shows through and will give the players clues.

The game is played by randomly spreading the 34 cards facedown. A child turns over one card and then tries to find its match. If the cards match and the child can read the word(s) on them, s/he gets to keep them. The child with the highest number of cards wins the game.

The words used for this activity were drawn from *Functional Reading,* vols. 1 and 2. These books, $3 each, are published by the Maryland State Department of Education (Publications Dept., Division of Instruction, P.O. Box 8717, Baltimore-Washington International Airport, Baltimore, MD 21240). They contain many valuable word lists and suggested student activities.

5. RECREATION

The recreational aspect of our world contains many print materials, such as game directions, sports articles, menus, and movie schedules. The most often read recreational material is probably the TV schedule. Whatever the educational value of TV, children's interest in it can be capitalized on.

One seventh-grade teacher developed a "TV Station" using back issues of *TV Guide* as references. In addition to providing youngsters with a creative writing exercise, this station forces them to compress and summarize their thoughts. One student went on to write a script for an episode of *I Love Lucy*. One set of directions for the station appears below.

Read this description of the television show:

② ❸ ⑩ ⑫ WELCOME BACK, KOTTER

Gabe gets worried when the sweathogs don leather jackets and affect street swaggers to defend their tough-guy reputation against a rival gang. Gabe: Gabriel Kaplan. Woodman: Sylvester White. Barbarino: John Travolta. Epstein: Robert Hegyes. Horshack: Ron Palillo. Washington: Lawrence-Hilton Jacobs. Carvelli: Charles Fleischer. Julie: Marcia Strassman. (Repeat)

Select five of the following TV shows: *Happy Days, Laverne and Shirley, Wonder Woman, The Waltons, Gilligan's Island, Starsky and Hutch, M.A.S.H., Little House on the Prairie, Sixty Minutes, I Love Lucy*. Make up a one-sentence description of an episode you would like to see telecast. Write it exactly as it might appear in *TV Guide*.

6. CITIZENSHIP

In order to be a good citizen, whether in a school, community, state, or nation, there are certain materials that a person must be able to read. Many elementary schools and most middle schools and junior highs have student handbooks. These usually describe a student's rights and responsibilities as well as provide some general information about the school. Many teachers have developed survival activities based on these student handbooks.

On another level, students must be able to read and understand specific vocabulary associated with their own local, state, and national governments. One fifth-grade teacher took the basic idea of the "Road to Survival" game and made her own "Democracy Derby." The students are given a list of words and their definitions to learn. When they finish, they can play "Democracy Derby."

The game board is pasted on the inside of a manila folder and then laminated. You will also need a die, several buttons, and a number of cards with words on one side and their definitions on the other. Words included are *democracy, polling place, legislature, representative, senator, Congress, vote, politics, political party, independence, capitalism, economy, president, Supreme Court, rights, bylaws, Constitution, local government,* and *foreign affairs.* To be sure students understand the words rather than simply memorize one set definition, there are two similar definitions worded slightly differently for each word. As a variation, you might add other definitions for some of the words to expose students to different connotations of these words.

Following are the directions:

1. Each player (limit, four players) chooses a button and places it at the starting line.

2. Make a card pile, putting the definitions faceup and the words facedown. Roll the die and draw the top card. Read the definition on it. Decide which of the words on your list is being defined. (Check your answer by looking on the back of the card.)

3. If you are correct, move the number of spaces on the die.

4. The first person to reach the finish line wins.

BEGIN SURVIVAL READING EARLY

Survival reading is an important part of any reading program. Attempts to include such matter in the curriculum have shown that students of all ages are interested in reading materials relevant to their own lives. There is no reason to reserve survival reading for the high school.

Reading for Special Occasions

by Nicholas P. Criscuolo

Holidays and special occasions are times which most children and adults look forward to eagerly. There are a variety of fun-filled school and social activities which these special days generate. Holidays also provide opportunities for children to read because reading can add an extra dimension to the excitement of holiday time.

How can teachers capitalize on this excitement? By taking from the theme of the special occasion and then launching a host of activities which highlight this theme. In order to offer concrete examples, this article will describe 12 fun-filled activities which center around the following holidays and special occasions: Christmas, St. Valentine's Day, St. Patrick's Day, Thanksgiving, Lincoln's Birthday, Washington's Birthday, Halloween, and Easter. Because these special occasions can be made even more exciting through free reading, this article will also cite two children's books that highlight the theme of each holiday.

1. CHRISTMAS STOCKING

Books read during the Christmas season can be noted appropriately by having the children write brief reports on white paper pasted to a Christmas stocking made from red construction paper trimmed with holly berries and poinsettia designs. Children can also prepare a Christmas Shopping List by consulting various catalogs, checking different lists, and examining the bibliographies which appear in such periodicals as the *Booklist, Horn Book,* and *School Library Journal*. Each of these titles will provide the names of many books they would like either to own personally or have access to in their school and/or classroom libraries.

2. CHRISTMAS SCENES

Preparing a Christmas play can be lots of fun and reinforce reading skills at the same time. Have the children read a story in their basal text or trade book that has a Christmas theme and then have them turn it into a play. The following format will prove helpful:

Scene	Location	Characters	Action
1	Jan's House	Jan Eddie	Eddie and Jan to visit Mr. Lake at his store. They want to buy a Xmas present for their mother.
2	Mr. Lake's Store	Jan Eddie Mr. Lake	Eddie and Jan look over Mr. Lake's merchandise. They don't see anything they like. Mr. Lake makes a suggestion.

Using this approach, a logical outline of the story's events will take shape. Parts can then be assigned and scenery made by the children. The students will also have fun making up appropriate dialog for each scene depicted.

Suggestions for Further Reading

1. Barth, Edna. *Holly, Reindeer, and Colored Lights*. New York: Seabury Press, 1971.
2. Cooney, Barbara. *Christmas*. New York: Crowell, 1967.

3. VALENTINE MESSAGES

Children who enjoyed a particular book can send a Valentine to the author. Pupils can fold a red piece of art paper in half to make it into a card. They can then cut a white sheet of paper into a Valentine, write a message to the author, and paste it on the folder card. An example:

Dear _____,
I enjoyed reading "The Mystery of the Hidden Door." It held my interest and I thought it had a lot of interesting characters. My favorite was Mike Kane because he was able to solve the mystery.
I like the ending very much. It was quite a surprise!

Sincerely,
Billy Jenkins

4. VALENTINE VERSES

Children enjoy sending each other Valentines. Put each class member's name on individual slips of paper and have each child draw a name. This will assure that everyone in the class will receive at least one Valentine.

Ask the children to write a verse to the individual whose name was drawn. This verse must be original and should try to incorporate something positive and unique about that individual. For example:

I know you like candy
As a person you're a dandy
You play football well too
I'm happy to send this
Valentine to you!

These verses can be mounted on cards which should be individually designed and decorated. Children will enjoy receiving these specially prepared Valentine verses.

Suggestions for Further Reading

1. Bulla, Clyde Robert. *St. Valentine's Day*. New York: Crowell, 1965.
2. Guilfoile, Elizabeth. *Valentine's Day*. Champaign, IL: Garrard, 1965.

5.   TURKEY FEATHERS

Turkey is something we associate with Thanksgiving Day, and it's a symbol that can be used to reinforce vocabulary. Pass out paper for a large cut-circle face and small light-colored paper to shape into headdress feathers. With crayon or magic marker, have children write a word to be reinforced on each feather.

After everyone has completed the head, have the children turn it over and draw a picture of a turkey on the plain circle. The headdress now becomes tail feathers. Children will have fun adding and "plucking" feathers on their turkeys as words are learned. Words of similar configuration are often troublesome for children, and these words lend themselves as feather words.

Suggestions for Further Reading

1. Barksdale, Lena. *The First Thanksgiving*. New York: Knopf, 1942.
2. Dalgliesh, Alice. *The Thanksgiving Story*. New York: Scribner, 1954.

6.   SHAMROCK PEOPLE

Many Irish personalities have made contributions to poetry, songs, theater, and so on. Invite pupils to first make bright green shamrocks by cutting out three identical hearts. They can paste the hearts so that only their tips are touching. A stem line can be drawn down from that point.

Let pupils select one Irish personality and write a short biographical sketch of that person on white paper. Make appropriate reference material available for this task. When completed, the finished sketch can be pasted onto the green shamrock.

Suggestions for Further Reading

1. Cantwell, Mary. *St. Patrick's Day*. New York: Crowell, 1967.
2. Sechrist, Elizabeth H. *Red Letter Days—A Book of Holiday Customs*. Turbotville, PA: Macrae Smith, 1965.

7. WASHINGTON'S VISIT

Many students have heard the statement "Washington slept here." Have them imagine that they lived in the colonies at that time, and that Washington visited their community in his travels.

Ask the children to write a creative story detailing the experiences of having such an illustrious visitor sleep in their home. Questions such as the following might stimulate their imaginations:

"How did Washington get there?"

"What were some things he said and did while in your home?"

"Where was he planning to go after he left your home?"

Some pupils may wish to do some research to accompany their creative stories by plotting on a map of the original colonies some of the actual places Washington was known to have visited as recorded by history.

8. RULES OF THE DAY

When George Washington was a boy, he copied in his notebook rules of behavior from a book called *Rules of Civility*. One of these rules was "Turn not your Back to others especially in Speeches, Tog not the Table or Desk on which another reads or writes, lean not upon anyone."

Ask pupils to translate these rules into today's language and to interpret them. Do they still hold true today? After this discussion, encourage them to write some important rules in their notebooks and then to share them with each other.

Suggestions for Further Reading

1. McNeer, May. *The Story of George Washington*. Nashville, TN: Abingdon, 1973.
2. North, Sterling. *George Washington; Frontier Colonel*. New York: Random House, 1957.

9. THE GREAT DEBATE

Organize a Lincoln-Douglas debate. There were many issues during Lincoln's time, e.g., slavery, which served as a basis for these famous debates. Have youngsters research these issues in preparation for the debates.

Select two children: one to appear as Abraham Lincoln and another as Stephen Douglas. Have them write down on index cards some of the points both debaters might have made, particularly as they related to the slavery issue.

If possible, ask "Mr. Douglas" and "Mr. Lincoln" to appear as people dressed in those days in order to add flavor to the debate.

10. SILHOUETTE SUMMARIES

Enable the pupils to discover several biographies of Abraham Lincoln. Have pupils select one well-known incident in his life, e.g., the hours preceding his assassination at Ford's Theater in Washington, D.C.

Have children compare the treatment of this tragedy by the different biographers and write a summary of them. These summaries can be written on 5 x 7 file cards pasted to a construction paper profile silhouette of Lincoln's famous face.

These silhouette summaries can be mounted on the bulletin board. Invite students to read them and to detect similar and different facts mentioned by the biographers writing about the same incident in Lincoln's life.

Suggestions for Further Reading

1. d'Aulaire, Ingri. *Abraham Lincoln*. New York: Doubleday, 1957.
2. McGovern, Ann. *If You Grew Up with Abraham Lincoln*. New York: Four Winds, 1966.

11. HALLOWEEN FUN

Encourage children to compile individual lists of words commonly associated with Halloween: witch, jack-o-lantern, pumpkin, costume, goblin, spooks, etc. Children can use this list in the following ways: (1) write an individual, creative story with a Halloween theme using as many of these words as possible; (2) make up riddles using these words; (3) write as a group-project an original story using the "brainstorming" technique, incorporating as many Halloween words as possible; and (4) draw a sketch of an unusual Halloween costume, write a short description of it, and explain why such a costume was chosen.

Suggestions for Further Reading

1. Barth, Edna. *Witches, Pumpkins, and Grinning Ghosts.* New York: Seabury, 1972.
2. Cooper, Paulette. *Let's Find Out about Halloween.* New York: Franklin Watts, 1972.

12. EASTER BASKETS

Each child's Easter Basket will grow when books are read and added to the basket in the form of eggs constructed of paper of different colors. Prior to initiating this holiday activity, discuss with the children the criteria for rating books. Have children then assign colors to these ratings, i.e., Red—Excellent; Yellow—Good; Blue—Fair; and so on. Every time the child reads a book, an egg is added to the Eastern Basket using a different color to represent the rating s/he has given it.

Suggestions for Further Reading

1. Barth, Edna. *Lillies, Rabbits and Painted Eggs.* New York: Seabury, 1970.
2. Fisher, Aileen. *Easter.* New York: Crowell, 1968.

This article has described twelve fun-filled activities for a sampling of holidays and special occasions. There are many more special occasions and many more activities which can be initiated with equal success. It's essential that teachers capitalize on the spirit of these days and enhance them by including reading as part of the festivities. These activities will enrich reading skills and add to the enjoyment of these special occasions.

PART
III

PROGRAMS

Introduction

Outstanding reading programs are numerous. Obviously, it is not possible to include the many accounts of successful experiences being reported in professional journals. Each article in this section describes types of programs which are considered to be among the most widely used and which represent an approach to motivating students to read through a central theme or thrust rather than a more general collection of activities.

The desire of children to read *real books* is the thesis behind the increased attention given to using literature rather than *readers* in reading instruction. In tune with the literature emphasis, Judith Wagner reports a program based on author awareness. "Call an Author" is an account of one school librarian's successful effort to acquaint middle school students with well-known authors via telephone interview. She details the procedures involved in the program and provides a reference for further information.

Other programs using reading sources other than basal readers are programs employing television scripts, a picture gallery, paperback books, and student-written books. In "An Interview with a Pioneer" Rosemary Lee Potter describes Michael McAndrew's television script-reading project in the Philadelphia schools. This report traces the development of the program, emphasizes the philosophy behind it, and shows the positive effects it has had in motivating students to read. Nicholas P. Criscuolo, in "Six Simple Crafts for Remedial Reading," explains how to go about designing an effective remedial reading program that will appeal to students who have been frustrated by repeated failures. A picture gallery is one of the crafts which he uses to show how to motivate the reluctant reader. Wide use of paperbacks in classrooms, media centers, and the home is becoming an accepted practice especially with the rising cost of hardcover books. Mary Eble and Jeanne Renton describe a paperback program in "Books Unlimited: A School-Wide Reading Program." They discuss the implementation of the program, methods of recording completed readings, and reflections of both students and teachers. A sampling of paperback titles used in the program includes brief annotations and student comments. Ann B. Madison gives the details of a program based on books written and illustrated by the students themselves. "Read and Rock—A Special Kind of Reading Center" reveals the value of such a center in developing reading abilities and attitudes.

A number of articles describe directed individualized reading. One of the most comprehensive is "Getting Kids Into Books: The Importance of Individualized Reading" by Terry C. Ley. The author briefly explains the current research findings about reading and the adolescent "which can assist teachers seeking ways to encourage both skill development and lifetime reading habits in their students." He then provides the reader with specific information on operating an individualized reading program. In "How to Set Up and Evaluate a DIR Program" Ley discusses in detail the selection process of finding books, setting up and evaluating the program, and the numerous benefits to be realized.

Call an Author

by Judith Wagner

Pat Scales has vivid childhood recollections of school libraries as gray halls of ominous silence, dutifully patrolled by librarians whose eyebrows rose at the drop of a sound. She remembers camouflaging comic books behind the august covers of classics and encyclopedias. And talking in whispers with a friend among dimly lit stacks to escape the smothering "shushhh" from frowning librarians or hatching endless conspiracies with classmates to disrupt the heavy quiet with all kinds of monkey business.

Today Ms. Scales is herself a school librarian at Greenville Middle School in Greenville, South Carolina, and she has not forgotten the stifling silence or the fastidious librarians. In organizing a program to help sixth-, seventh-, and eighth-grade students find a more positive attitude toward reading, she has built the activities around one premise: that libraries should be places where students are free to explore and discover the vast world of children's literature. The premise is firmly supported by the Greenville Middle School administration and faculty.

Of course, Ms. Scales would be the first to concede that times have changed. Those shush-ing librarians of her childhood have given way to a new breed often called media specialists and what used to be a room with books on shelves and some tables and chairs is changing into a full-service media or resource center. But the name changes are only surface signs. "Even more significant," says Ms. Scales, "are the changes in the underlying philosophy of school libraries. The librarian no longer works in isolation but as a part of the teaching team. Equally important, the inhibiting silence of yesterday's libraries has been replaced by the natural, positive sounds of children asking questions, pulling out the card catalog trays, thumbing through books or magazines, and peering at slides or listening to records."

A premise, Ms. Scales strongly feels, should be put into practice. In the Greenville school library, students *are* free to explore and discover children's literature. Much of the middle schoolers' stepped-up interest in reading stems from a project she undertook to entice the youngsters—from slow to gifted readers—to read more, venture into broader areas, and develop a more critical eye for the printed page. The project's influence has gone beyond the original reading goal. For example, Greenville teachers notice that those ho-hum book reports beginning ''I like this book because. . .'' are on the decline.

Ms. Scales' idea was ingeniously simple: Why not arrange for a series of telephone calls to leading authors of children's books and let a group of students ask them questions? Thanks to the rental of a conference unit set to handle group conversations, full cooperation from the school staff, and Ms. Scales' cost-conscious planning, the project has caught on. Any possible technical and operational snags were ironed out in the project's planning stages with assistance from a telephone company representative.

Behind a successful project is hard work and planning. Ms. Scales, the school staff, and students have been willing to map out and carry through each phase of the project with a careful eye on details. As a first step, Ms. Scales gathers with teachers and students to select authors whose works will be read and studied with some depth in the regular classes. No student is required to participate in the project, but those who want to take part in an interview must read at least one book by the author.

Next, Ms. Scales and the students write letters requesting phone interviews. Most of the authors respond quickly and only a few of the requests have actually gone unanswered. So far, only one author has refused an interview. The letter of request makes it clear that no honorarium can be given for the interview. Again, the authors have been understanding. One author—award-winning juvenile novelist Natalie Babbitt—had this reaction: ''Anyone who would expect an honorarium for such a pleasant experience should leave writing and go into usury.'' Not letting an opportunity slip by, Ms. Scales and her cooperating teachers used Ms. Babbitt's response as a springboard for discussion among the students about why some authors willingly share their time with young readers while others ignore their letters, what pressure writers face at a particular time, and what realities of public relations prevail in the publishing industry.

Two weeks before an interview is scheduled, students give Ms. Scales questions which they would like to ask the author. Since interviews run between 20 and 30 minutes and the time goes fast, only a few of these questions can actually be used. Inevitably, competition is keen among the students to see who can come up with meaty inquiries.

The so-called usual questions also have their place in the interview. For example, how did the author get the idea for a particular story? Does he or she write at a designated time every day or wait for an idea to come? What were the author's favorite books as a youngster? What are his or her hobbies? Does the author have children? The questions are handy indices for the students. ''By repeating these questions with several authors,'' says Ms. Scales, ''students can get a good perspective on individual differences and preferences, even within the same profession. It begins to occur to them that there are many ways of being creative with words and ideas.''

One question students frequently want to ask is what would have happened to a particular character if the story had continued beyond its current ending. Ms. Scales and the language arts teachers capitalize on this curiosity as a means for generating creative writing and dramatic activities.

When students develop their lists of possible questions, they are encouraged to think about the author's particular style of writing and method of characterization. They are invited to delve into similarities and differences within the author's works and to draw comparisons with other writers they have studied. ''Sometimes students will discover an inconsistency in the story or a factual error,'' says Ms. Scales. ''Although we guide them in designing polite ways to ask the question, we don't stop them from inquiring. After all, these young people, as consumers of juvenile literature, have every right to question its quality and factual content.''

To date, Elaine Konigsburg, Judy Blume, Betsy Byars, William Armstrong, Natalie Babbitt, Irene Hunt, and Bill and Vera Cleaver are among the noted writers who have been interviewed. Each has been articulate and responsive during the telephone sessions and several have followed up with letters to the students, exploring various questions in detail or picking up a point overlooked during the phone conversation.

Sometimes an author responds to student queries with pat answers, probably because the questions have been asked them over and over again and answers come too automatically. However, in several instances, authors have expressed surprise and delight at the depth and perceptiveness of student inquiries. One of the project's lighter moments occurred when seventh grader David Ghighi earnestly asked the husband-wife writing team of Vera and Bill Cleaver if they ever fought over story ideas.

During an interview, between 20 and 25 students actually speak with the author, with up to 150 more listening in. The large numbers are easily handled by a Model 50-A portable telephone conference unit which has an amplifier and two microphones. The only extra equipment needed to accommodate the unit is a telephone jack.

According to Grace Gibson, school representative for the telephone company in Greenville, charges for renting the equipment vary throughout the country, ranging from about $11 to $16 per month plus a one-time installation fee. The only additional cost to schools is the bill for the long-distance calls. However, Ms. Scales is able to hold down the tab by organizing questions ahead of time, prearranging exact time for interviews, and dialing direct. Long-distance charges in the Greenville program have averaged between $6 and $7 per interview. ''Personally, I can't think of a more economical way in the world for 175 students to meet leading writers,'' contends Ms. Scales.

The interviews have a way of grabbing student interest. Even the students who were left out because they didn't finish the book they were supposed to have read for the interview are often turned on by post-interview excitement among their classmates who did earn the chance to participate. "Many spend free periods or time after school listening to a tape of the interview, and they are usually the first to knuckle down in order to participate in the next round," points out Ms. Scales.

There are many signs beyond student and faculty enthusiasm that the program is effective. Students have become *author-conscious* in their reading; book circulation at the Greenville Middle School has jumped about 50 percent since the project began. "Books are not just leaving the library destined for a two-week stash at the back of someone's locker," explains Ms. Scales. "Students now want to talk about what they have read and in much greater detail than the 'I liked the book because. . . .' routine."

Although the project's direct impact upon improved reading skills is unknown, reading and English teachers and the library staff have observed that both advanced and less skilled readers are selecting more varied and challenging books for independent reading. "My philosophy," says Ms. Scales, "is that the more children read, the better they read. Some of the slower readers are reading more; we're hoping that the increase will have a direct and lasting effect upon their skills."

There are other encouraging signs. At a recent school book fair, sales of books by authors interviewed under the project were higher by far than books which are normally top-sellers at such events. And student enthusiasm has also reached home. Several parents have volunteered to help Ms. Scales and the teachers with preparation details in exchange for an invitation to attend the interviews.

The project has had an important effect on general communication. Students, teachers, and library workers agree that the experience of planning and working together for the interviews has fostered an esprit de corps and made it easier to communicate among one another at other levels.

The end of an interview does not mean the end of interest in the author. "You might think, once an interview is completed, that would be *it* for a particular author," says Ms. Scales. "Not so. We try to look at the interviews as one exciting part of a whole process and as a means for more learning." Follow-up activities often include student-made filmstrips, transparencies, audiotapes, bulletin boards, and scrapbooks. Students are further encouraged to tie in the fiction they have read with subjects drawn from other academic disciplines like history, social studies, and science.

The project has stretched beyond the original language arts focus and now includes interested elementary school students and a life science class in a middle school which plans to study and interview two fiction writers who use their own knowledge of nature as a backdrop for their stories. In the future, Ms. Scales hopes to expand the interview concept to include an interdisciplinary approach to conversations with public officials, people in the news, national authorities on subjects of interest to students, and candidates for public office. Another possibility entails interviewing members of various professions to help students in making career decisions. "The possibilities are limitless," points out Ms. Scales. "Everywhere I go someone comes up with a promising variation on the telephone-interview theme. Our school library is rarely quiet these days." With sounds productive rather than disruptive, no one is about to say "shushhh" to that.

An Interview with a Pioneer

by Rosemary Lee Potter

Seven years ago, when I was teaching a second-grade class, I read about Michael McAndrew and his television script-reading project in the Philadelphia schools. His reported success with the program was one of the reasons I decided on graduate study in television *use* with children. Several months ago I heard McAndrew speak to a group of Pinellas County (Clearwater, FL) reading teachers. This interview began that day. (McAndrew is Director of Educational Services, Capital Cities Television Productions in Philadelphia.)

Potter: When and how did the television script-reading project you are currently directing begin? What were and are you trying to do?
McAndrew: The Television Reading Program began nine years ago in a senior high school in Philadelphia. I was an English teacher working with eleventh- and twelfth-grade students whose abilities ranged from modest to outstanding. They were grouped homogeneously. I became frustrated at the difficulty most students had with reading because of an apparent lack of basic skills. Another frightening factor was some students' obvious apathy toward reading of any kind. Maybe this was the overpowering problem—motivating those who could read but preferred not to. Trying to reach children who have little interest, limited vocabularies, and few comprehension skills is no easy task. And naturally, students who cannot read well usually do not perform well in other areas, such as social studies, math, and science.

My students seemed to be as disappointed as I was. Many wanted to read. They wanted to become more involved with the world of the printed word. What to do? I finally hit upon the idea of combining the electronic medium that occupies so much of their time with its printed form, the television script. In the beginning, I used actual television tapes of commercial programs, such as "Lucy," "Ironside," and "Brian's Song," along with their television scripts, which I had acquired from the programs' executive producers.
Potter: How did the children react?

McAndrew: The immediate response was overwhelming. The students began reading, interacting, writing, and developing creative skills as they wrote original scripts. Their reading scores rose dramatically. Students who had been having trouble with reading were saying, "I don't know how to read this, but I want to"—the first stage, obviously. One parent of a child who was able to read, but who had chosen to spend little time reading said, "I don't know how much these scripts cost, but I wish to subscribe. My son has become excited about reading again, and we don't want this phenomenon to stop."

Potter: Describe the expansion of the original idea.

McAndrew: The cost of producing videotapes prohibited expansion of the original Television Reading Program. Then, national press coverage of the program resulted in inquiries from approximately 4,000 school systems throughout the country, from New York City to a Navajo reservation. I experimented to see if the motivation would be as intense without the videotapes. This led to a request to the three major networks and their executive producers for advance scripts of their programs. They all responded enthusiastically. Having scripts in advance, I soon discovered, increases student motivation. They were eager to read the scripts and do the accompanying exercises. It was as if we had tomorrow's newspaper today.

My next step was to expand the program and include television scripts in areas of study other than my English classes. With the full cooperation of Marjorie Farmer, Executive Director of Language Arts and Reading, and George French, Director of Social Studies (both of the Philadelphia school system), I experimented with such scripts as "Missiles of October," "Huck Finn," and "I'll Fight No More Forever." All three were used in an interdisciplinary manner. Each script was used in a slightly different fashion, but they all followed the same basic route: each time 1,600 secondary students participated; each time the students and their teachers received the scripts three weeks in advance of the program's presentation; and each time the students were allowed and encouraged to take the scripts home.

Potter: Did any parents comment on the fact that they were being encouraged to watch television by the school?

McAndrew: The interaction in the classrooms and at home was unprecedented. Parents and older relatives were as excited to get involved in the live action of the television scripts as were their children. One involved parent remarked, "We finally have something to talk about over the dinner table instead of the usual grunts and groans."

The question now arose: How could I involve more students and their families without additional expense for our school system? It seemed too simple! Publish the next script in one of our major Philadelphia newspapers. I chose "Eleanor and Franklin," a beautifully written television adaptation of Joseph Lash's best-selling novel. Lash allowed this "first," knowing that it might limit sales of his book in Philadelphia, the fourth largest book market in the United States.

The "Eleanor and Franklin" script, published in the *Philadelphia Inquirer* on January 9, 1976, went out to approximately one million readers, including 130,000 Philadelphia secondary school students. The response was tremendous. Our school and others throughout the city used the script in a variety of settings, particularly in the areas of language arts and social studies. Students and teachers, plus every reader of the *Inquirer*, had the script well in advance of its network airing. An interesting sidenote is that Lash's book sold out in the Philadelphia area. And school and public libraries reported numerous requests for not only Lash's book but also other books about the Roosevelts.

Potter: What is the current script-reading project at Capital Cities?

McAndrew: I believe the television script is a legitimate art form, one that is as real as the essay, the novel, the short story, and the play. To ignore television scripts is to ignore an opportunity to help students move into the world of the printed word. I believe that we must incorporate the use of television scripts into every curriculum throughout the country.

To help make this happen, I took a leave of absence from the Philadelphia public schools and became Director of Educational Services at Capital Cities Communications. With the encouragement and support of Daniel Burke, Capital Cities President, I have secured the complete cooperation of the three major networks—ABC, NBC, and CBS. They are providing a selection of scripts from which we choose those we think are appropriate for our Television Reading Program.

Our staff prepares teacher's guides concentrating on the development of vocabulary and comprehension skills to accompany each script. The program is meant to be used as a supplement to any existing school reading program.

Potter: Can you give us any feedback from this year's project?

McAndrew: The Capital Cities program is currently being piloted in Washington, DC, New York, Philadelphia and its suburbs, and the Archdiocese of Philadelphia. The full year's program, underwritten by Capital Cities, is being evaluated by Pennsylvania State University. As soon as we have collected some tangible results, we will make them available to the public.

So far the responses have been positive. Our first project was one of the episodes of the "Six Million Dollar Man." This was followed by episodes from "The Waltons" and "Little House on the Prairie." In the course of the full year's program we will use a total of 10 scripts with 10 accompanying guides. Participating students and teachers receive their materials two weeks before the program appears, and we encourage them to use the materials for several days after the program has been aired. The guides are based entirely on the content of the scripts. Actual viewing of the programs is not essential.

Initial responses from students and teachers suggest that this script-reading project may affect attitudes. In participating schools attendance is up substantially, discipline problems have decreased, free reading has increased, attitudes toward reading are changing positively, and written exercises seem more acceptable to the students. We all know that there is no panacea for current problems in reading. But we also know that the scripts have given teachers and students a new vehicle for skill development, one that is limited only by the imagination of the user.

Potter: How do you explain the apparent cooperation and/or change of attitude among parents, teachers, and media personnel regarding this script-reading idea? Doesn't this conflict with the current furor about television's "bad effect" on children and their reading habits?

McAndrew: Most educators seem to agree that children and adults spend too much of their leisure time watching television, leading to alienation from the world of reading for some. Many critics simply criticize television without understanding and accepting its tremendous potential for education. Script-reading allows us to explore television along with our students and even their parents. By recognizing and using the art form of television scripts, we can become more selective, more demanding and, ultimately, more literate. It seems only natural that this study should begin in our nation's classrooms.

Potter: What does the future hold?

McAndrew: The printed art form of television has come of age. Within the next few years I see it as an integral part of the educational scene. Scripts will be regularly printed in newspapers throughout the world, expanding this influential medium into an outstanding educational arm of the community. I believe that attitudes toward television will change and that better programming will result because a more sophisticated audience will make itself heard.

The entire community can benefit from the script-reading experience. Perhaps there will be a renewed interest in reading and writing, especially in the schools. And the skeptics might finally come around to seeing the great horizons that television can open up for a literate society.

Six Simple Crafts for Remedial Reading

by Nicholas P. Criscuolo

Designing an effective remedial reading program is challenging because it must create a desire for learning in someone who has experienced failure. Approaches that use a variety of media can be effective. They not only get results in helping students acquire basic reading skills, but also allow them to experience pleasure and satisfaction in reading—feelings that many of these students have never had.

In designing a quality remedial reading program, there are many factors to consider: length and frequency of remedial sessions, size of remedial reading groups, and the content of the program. The last factor is by far the most important. It is essential to get the remedial reader interested in developing reading skills that have been presented but not mastered.

The approaches used in the remedial reading program must be fresh, creative, and involve the learner's active participation. Materials and techniques must be appealing and effective. The most effective approaches not only stimulate interest, but also involve all the senses and different learning styles. Following are six AV approaches to remedial reading.

PICTURE GALLERY

Children can be photographed in a variety of poses and school activities. These pictures can then be used to motivate readers by having them write a short commentary or text to accompany each picture. The pictures can form a bulletin board display called the picture gallery, or be exchanged among the learners. The text-photos can also be put into a scrapbook and placed in the reading folder for supplementary reading.

To sharpen vocabulary skills (this is often a deficit among poor readers), pictures of people can be clipped out of magazines and descriptive words used to characterize the facial expressions of the people in the pictures. For example, rather than use such overworked words as *pretty,* *beautiful,* or *tired,* the students can be encouraged to use such words as *serene, weary,* or *enchanting.*

UNFINISHED STORIES

For remedial readers, it is important to integrate skills in order to provide maximum reinforcement and support. Reading and writing skills can be developed by providing short paragraphs that are beginnings of stories. Students are asked to read these story-starters and then write endings for them.

Story-starters can also take the form of pictures. The children look at the pictures, choose one that interests them, and write a story to go along with the picture.

Story beginnings can also be taped. Children love to use the tape recorder and—for remedial readers, who tend to be easily distracted—earphones. They listen to these taped stories and then either record or write endings for them.

MUSICAL SOUNDS AND MESSAGES

Most children like music. After getting copyright clearance, duplicate and distribute the lyrics of popular songs to the class. A variety of phonics and comprehension activities can be accomplished with these sheets.

Both classical and popular music can be played in the classroom, with the students encouraged to use less common words to describe the sounds they hear (i.e., *tranquil, eerie, strident*).

As a further reinforcer of aural skills, a listening post can be set up with tape recordings, records, and cassette players in either classroom or reading laboratory. The idea of *loan phones* (two-way phones set up so that students can arrange to borrow books) has appeal.

PROP BAGS

Getting remedial readers to read voluntarily is not always easy. And getting them to report on what they read is even harder. To add interest to oral reports, students can go through a story or book they have read and make a list of some of the physical objects mentioned. These objects can be obtained or made up from a variety of materials—bits of cloth, cardboard, and so on—and placed in a prop bag. As the report is being given, the youngster fishes into the prop bag for the appropriate object and displays it to the group. This sharpens visual memory skills and enhances oral book reporting.

Remedial readers can use other materials and media in reporting on reading done. For example, they can make a soap or balsa wood carving of a scene or character. They can make stand-up characters or puppets and design costumes for them. They can make a collage or construct a wire mobile or build a scale model of an important object in the story or book.

TV SCRIPTS

Many children like to watch television and can be motivated to read the scripts of some programs. The CBS Television Reading Program has been instrumental in this kind of activity. CBS stations air such specials as "A Circle of Children" or "The Defection of Simas Kudirka." Scripts of the shows are made available for children to read before or during the telecast. A teacher's manual contains many activities for reinforcing reading skills in all subject areas.

This kind of program works especially well for remedial readers because it uses a potent learning tool—television—and combines it with many techniques that stress the acquisition of reading skills.

PERSONAL EXPERIENCE STORIES

Even though a youngster is classified as a remedial reader, this does not mean that he or she has not had a great many different experiences. One of the best devices to use with remedial readers is the personal experience story. Students are encouraged to tell about some of their experiences. These are written down by the teacher and then typed with a title and the author's name added. Students illustrate the stories using a variety of media. Students are especially interested in reading material they themselves have created. The stories can be compiled into class anthologies and collections to be read by the other members of the class.

As an added feature, the author can select his or her favorite story and tape it using sound effects. This type of activity not only reinforces reading skills, but also improves the self-image of the remedial reader.

Books Unlimited: A School-Wide Reading Program

by Mary Eble
and Jeanne Renton

Before teachers can convince students of the importance of reading, they must first introduce them to the pleasure of reading. A federally funded project enabled teachers at Fairview High School in Fairview Park, Ohio to do just this. With the purchase of $3500 worth of paperbacks, we launched a school-wide reading program, "Books Unlimited," with one main theme: every student a reader. The two major goals of the program were to give students the skills they need to read well and to provide literary experiences which will increase students' appreciation of reading.

Our specific objectives were (1) to broaden students' frames of reference; (2) to improve students' self-image; (3) to help students better understand themselves and their relationships with others; (4) to increase students' vocabularies; (5) to encourage students to seek additional information about specific areas of interest; (6) to help students express feelings through small group discussion; (7) to expose students to the joy of reading.

Paperbacks are suitable for a school-wide program such as this because they are colorful and attractive, easy to carry, inexpensive, and have a special student appeal. We selected paperbacks on a variety of subjects from car racing to cloning, and spanning a wide range of reading levels. Multiple copies of "tried and true" titles were included, such as *The Magician*, *The Pigman*, *Hatter Fox* and *Deathwatch*. We purchased for all grade levels those titles with universal appeal, for example, *Catch a Killer*, *Dove*, *Brian's Song*, *If I Love You Am I Trapped Forever?*, *Karen*, and *Just Dial a Number*. (A sampling of the titles purchased for the program is included at the end of this article.)

The circulation procedure was as painless as possible—no fines, no reading deadlines. We encouraged a one-week loan, but this was open to modification based on consultations with each student concerning his/her special needs.

The program was introduced through all the English and reading classes, and each teacher was involved in planning, implementing, and evaluating the program. As an important part of the curriculum, Books Unlimited gave teachers an opportunity to observe students in a freer setting, to discover new titles, and to include activities related to the program in their lesson plans.

A library media specialist was in charge of each of the three grade level areas: grades seven and eight, grades nine and ten, grades eleven and twelve. This setup resulted in individualized attention, service, and selection.

One important aspect of the program was the students' responses to each book read. Students wrote the book's author, title, and a short comment on small review cards. Seventh and eighth graders were asked merely to react to the book, ninth and tenth graders included point of view, and eleventh and twelfth graders were expected to pick out the theme and express it in a sentence or two. Reviews were filed in the library media center for teacher and student use. The students found them to be quite helpful when selecting titles.

A permanent record card was filled out for each student and all books read were recorded. Upon request, cards belonging to seniors could be placed in the student's permanent record file.

EVALUATING THE PROGRAM

We evaluated the reading program after the first year and arrived at these conclusions.

1. All students can read if appropriate materials are provided.

2. Most students will read if stimulated with the "first good book no one makes you read."

3. Many students need personal attention to get them started.

4. Some students need recommendations at first but will soon begin selecting books independently.

5. Students are interested in what other students say about books.

6. The reading and comprehension abilities of many students are often underestimated.

7. Many students can read between the lines, carefully extracting the theme of the book.

8. Most students try to relate literature to their own lives and feelings.

9. The record card where students listed the titles they had read was useful to teachers, important to other students, and assisted the library media specialists with selection.

10. A personalized reading program may help reach the so-called turned-off student.

11. The program was completely voluntary and, therefore, we were quite pleased that approximately 70 percent of our 1800 students in grades seven through twelve participated in the project.

12. Several teachers (especially those in charge of study halls) noticed a great increase in reading among students.

13. Many of the more prolific readers were not necessarily the most successful academic students.

14. Some students who had never completed a book on their own not only finished a book but also read several others.

Books Unlimited has become an established program of our library media center, setting the stage for other programs that have evolved out of the interest and commitment of the English teachers and the library media staff. These include scheduled visits once or twice a month to the library media center so that classes can select books and read quietly; photo-essays; small group discussions; reading ladder selections (the names of books on a common theme are placed on the rungs of a ladder, one title to a rung; as one "goes up the ladder," the books increase in reading difficulty and maturational level); teaching book reviewing techniques; bibliographies annotated by students.

TEACHERS COMMENT

Because of Books Unlimited, more students are reading more books with more enthusiasm. Teachers' comments attest to the success of the program.

"Students began to carry their books with them and quite often used the books to fill time before class or after assignments were completed."

". . . students began to enjoy reading."

"Several times I heard students say, 'This is the first book I've ever finished.' What a good feeling that gave me."

"Multiple copies of many books as well as extensive examples of various genres allowed me, as a teacher, to utilize the library material for small classroom discussions and individualized critiques on a single subject or author."

"Book selections were diverse enough to permit success at all levels."

"The Books Unlimited reading program is outstanding in helping reluctant readers to do more than they have ever done before. I have seen these results."

"Reading reports done by students placed the emphasis of the program on reading and not on the report itself."

SAMPLING OF PAPERBACK TITLES PURCHASED FOR BOOKS UNLIMITED READING PROGRAM

(The quoted statements following each annotation are student comments taken from the review cards.)

Grades 7-8

Bellairs, John. *The House with a Clock in Its Walls*.

A wicked magician has set a magic clock to ring and usher in the destruction of the world. "Superb! Excellent mystery and suspense. Really captures the imagination. Great ending."

Clarke, Arthur. *2001: A Space Odyssey*.

Hal, an insane computer, tries to kill the astronauts in this story of a space voyage of the future. "Exciting; very good science fiction."

Colman, Hilda. *Diary of a Frantic Kid Sister*.

Sarah is positive her mother favors her older sister, Didi. "Great. I just loved it. It is very real and you can identify with the girl's problems."

Crichton, Michael. *The Andromeda Strain*.

A virus from outer space threatens earth. "This was the best science fiction book I've read yet! It was believable and really good."

Danziger, Paula. *The Cat Ate My Gymsuit*.

Marcy supports a controversial teacher and finds herself suspended from school. "It was really terrific! It's got all types of sensitivity, humor, sadness and happiness. I'd love to read more of her stories."

Duncan, Lois. *Down a Dark Hall*.

Girls in a private school have the terrifying experience of being "used" by dead geniuses from the past. "This book was a real spine chiller! I really enjoyed it and am anxious to take out her other books."

Green, Bette. *Summer of My German Soldier*.

A young Jewish girl shows great courage and compassion in hiding an escaped Nazi prisoner of war. "I liked it because it showed that girls can have guts, too."

Gunther, John. *Death Be Not Proud*.

John Gunther's memorial to his 18-year-old son who died of a brain tumor. "A truly touching book. I really enjoyed reading it and couldn't put it down."

Head, Ann. *Mr. & Mrs. Bo Jo Jones.*

Bo Jo and July are hardly ready to assume adult responsibilities following their hasty wedding. "I think this book was terrific. I would like to see more books like it."

Hinton, S.E. *The Outsiders.*

Teenagers divide into rival gangs, the Socs and the Greasers. "It was so good that I read it in one night."

Hinton, S.E. *That Was Then, This Is Now.*

A hopeless drug addiction disrupts the friendship between Mark and Bryon. "Best book ever written. I cried right through but I still couldn't put it down. S.E. Hinton, please write more!"

Madison, Winifred. *Growing Up in a Hurry.*

A shy girl experiences her first romance. "It was realistic. I enjoyed it very much."

Maxwell, Edith. *Just Dial a Number.*

Teenagers make a prank phone call which results in the deaths of a fellow student's parents. "This book kept you in suspense all the way to the end and made you never want to set it down."

Perry, Gaylord. *Me and the Spitter.*

Gaylord Perry reveals the secret league of spitball pitchers. "I like the book a lot because the person it was about was telling it. It wasn't boring in any part of the book."

Sherburn, Zoa. *Why Have the Birds Stopped Singing?*

Katie, who has epilepsy, bumps her head and is magically transported into the past where she is mistaken for her "crazy" great-great-grandmother. "I liked the book very much because it showed how hard it was to live in the past with the same disease we live easily with now."

Sleator, William. *Run.*

With no telephone, three teenagers huddle in fear when a robber-addict returns to their house. "I really liked this book. I felt like I was one of the characters in it."

Taylor, Theodore. *The Cay.*

Timothy and Philip are marooned on a cay, suffering many hardships before rescue comes. "This book was very interesting. I was glad to see it was in the first person. This makes it more personal. It went very quickly. The description of Timothy and the hurricane was detailed and good.''

Tolkien, J.R.R. *The Fellowship of the Ring*.

This is the first book of a trilogy of fantasy by the author of *The Hobbit*. ''It was a fantastic book!'' ''I liked it a lot.''

Van Leeuwen, Jean. *I Was a 90-Pound Duckling*.

Kath has typical problems of a girl who matures physically later than her friends. ''I thought it was a very good and funny book and enjoyed it very much.''

White, Robb. *Deathwatch*.

Ben fights a desperate battle for survival in the desert. ''I liked it because it had a lot of action.''

Wojciechowska, Maia. *Tuned Out*.

Kevin's drug dependence shatters his whole family. ''I liked the book.'' ''It showed the emotions of the family like it would be in life.''

Grades 9-10

Bailey, Maurice and Marilyn Bailey. *Staying Alive!*

Exciting account of survival in the sea for 117 days. ''A good story of survival.'' ''It got to me.''

Clark, Mary Higgins, *Where Are the Children?*

Ten years ago Nancy was accused of murdering her children—now she is experiencing the same nightmare again! ''They should make a movie out of it.'' ''You don't want to put it down.'' ''Good, and kept me in suspense.'' ''One of the better books I've read.'' ''A real shocker!'' ''It kept you on the edge of your chair.''

Cruz, Nicky. *Run, Baby, Run*.

This is the true account of Nicky Cruz, a young gang leader who made a decision to follow Christ and help other young people. ''Fast moving and interesting.'' ''Excellent.''

Duncan, Lois. *I Know What You Did Last Summer*.

Four teenagers try to keep their hit-and-run accident a secret—but someone else knows! ''A real thriller.'' ''Always some kind of action and suspense.'' ''I think teenagers should read this.''

Elfman, Blossom. *The Girls of Huntington House*.

A young woman decides to become a teacher in a home for unwed mothers. ''A funny, happy sad book.'' ''The book is very good because it shows that people still care that unwed mothers are people with feelings of their own.''

Farris, John. *When Michael Calls.*

Aunt Helen receives telephone calls from her nephew, Michael, but Michael has been dead for sixteen years. "Quite thrilling." "Never suspected the ending." "When I was done, I wished there was more."

Guy, Rosa. *The Friends.*

It's difficult to imagine Phyllissia and Edith as friends, but each fills a need in the other's life. "It moved very fast and I got involved with the main characters." "A very surprising book, very good, seemed real, a lot of it shocked me the way it turned out." "It was believable." "I thought it was a good book. It showed how prejudiced some people can be and yet how others really don't care what color, race or creed you are."

Hinton, S.E. *Rumble Fish.*

Fourteen-year-old Rusty James idolizes his older brother, but tragedy strikes and both brothers pay a price. "I recommend this to everyone." "Excellent—almost better than *The Outsiders.*"

Lipsyte, Robert. *The Contender.*

An aspiring young boxer prepares for a big fight and in the process finds a new maturity. "A fast moving book." "Excellent book." "An accurate definition of the word 'contender' in a form that you will not forget."

Lund, Doris. *Eric.*

Seventeen-year-old Eric, a leukemia victim, decides to live the rest of his life to the fullest. "Well-written." "I admired this man for his courage while dealing with his problem." "I enjoyed this book because of its sensitivity and its realistic outlook." "The book not only describes Eric's struggle to live but also his family and friends' fight to accept the fact of his death." "Outstanding, touching and fast moving." "I learned a lot."

Madison, Winifred. *Bird on the Wing.*

While hitchhiking, Elizabeth, a runaway, meets Maija, a weaver. Under Maija's influence, Elizabeth matures and achieves self-understanding. "You can't put it down." "The book shows how you can survive many things."

Mazer, Harry. *Snow Bound.*

Two young people survive for eleven days in the snow and learn to adjust and understand each other. "This book contains enjoyment and excitement for anyone reading it. Fast reading and very hard to put down."

Minahan, John. *Jeremy.*

Shy, fifteen-year-old Jeremy meets Susan and they fall in love. "They live in their own special world." "A tender love story." "I would recommend that everyone who likes love stories read *Jeremy.*"

Read, Piers Paul. *Alive.*

This survival story is about a plane full of young rugby players that crashes in the Andes. "I realize why they made the decisions they did, in order to stay alive." "A book you can't put down."

Sherburne, Zoa. *The Girl Who Knew Tomorrow.*

Sarah, who has the gift of ESP, becomes a well-known television star until she begins questioning her values. "Easy to read and understand." "I liked the book . . . interesting . . . well-written. You just keep reading so you find out what happens to her next." "It shows how ESP in one person can change many lives and how she changed her own." "You will really like this one."

Sherburne, Zoa. *Too Bad about the Haines Girl.*

A young girl faces the problems of telling her boyfriend and family about her pregnancy. "It dealt with problems of today." "It shows what a girl has to go through when pregnant." "Gives you insights into how she felt." "I liked the way it ended." "A book that taught a lesson." "Confide in your parents; they will love you no matter what."

Sleator, William. *House of Stairs.*

Five sixteen-year-old orphans find themselves in a large structure full of stairs while a strange machine attempts to control their actions. "It was really very strange. It built up to a very exciting climax and had a very odd ending." "A good psychological book." "I enjoyed playing a part in this book." "Hard to believe, but if you had an imagination, it was almost truth."

Smith, Betty. *Joy in the Morning.*

A very young and poor couple is determined to make a good life together. "One of the best love stories I have read." "*Joy in the Morning* is my favorite." "Their love is stronger than the forces opposing them." "It has humor as well as very real problems." "I really loved this book!"

Spiegel, Marshall. *The Cycle Jumpers.*

This story features two motorcycle daredevils, Evel Knievel and Gary

Wells. "I like this type of book and think there should be more like it." "Easy to read."

Valens, E.G. *The Other Side of the Mountain.*

Jill Kinmont becomes paralyzed in a skiing accident and courageously sets out to readjust her life-style. "Interesting and inspiring." "I thought the story was very good. It moved quickly and was very detailed. I felt like part of the story. I could really understand how Jill felt."

Vare, Robert. *Buckeye.*

This tells the exciting saga of Woody Hayes and the Ohio State football team. "Action-packed." "A quick moving sports story."

Walker, Margaret. *Jubilee.*

This story of the Civil War is written from a courageous Black woman's point of view. "Well-written." "This is part of American history and this book made it live for me."

Woolfolk, Dorothy. *"Murder, My Dear!"*

Eighteen-year-old Melissa takes a summer job as a companion to an old lady and soon finds herself involved in a dangerous situation. "Dorothy Woolfolk did a wonderful job in writing this book." "A great thriller. I will certainly read more books by this same author." "Exceptionally well written and full of suspense." "I had no idea who the killer was until the last few chapters." "One of the best murder mysteries I've ever read." "I read it in one sitting."

Zindel, Paul. *The Pigman.*

Paul and Loraine alternately tell the story of their relationship with Mr. Pignati. The old man's tragic death raises many questions for the young people to consider. "I was really involved in the book." "I liked this book because it showed human emotions and how people react to different situations." "I found this book to be witty, dramatic, and very moving." "I liked this book because something like this almost happened to me and I could really relate to this man's thoughts."

Grades 11-12

Baldwin, James. *If Beale Street Could Talk.*

A beautiful love story in which Baldwin gently tells of a young, pregnant girl and her innocently jailed lover. "Everything is so real and true to life, so honest and open, full of caring and understanding." "Even though an environment may be harsh and brutal, there is always love around."

Barjavel, Rene. *The Ice People*.

Scientists in Antarctica discover a man and a woman buried in ice for 900,000 years. They are the lone survivors of a superior civilization. "Among the best I've ever read." "The book raises the question can civilized man ever learn to survive himself or is destruction inevitable." "Kept me enthralled."

Brickhill, Paul. *The Great Escape*.

An astounding tale of the daring escape of British prisoners during World War II. "Excellent." "Exciting." "Keeps you in suspense all the way through."

Camus, Albert. *The Stranger*.

A Frenchman kills an Arab, stands trial and is condemned to die. "This excellent novel relies heavily on a theme which was reflected by the mundane day-to-day narrative." "A very deep novel." "The first part is brilliant background for an excellent philosophical second part."

Cormier, Robert. *The Chocolate War*.

When a high school student refuses to sell chocolate bars during the annual sale shocking things begin to happen. "One of the best books I have ever read." "Extremely well written." "You feel what is happening to the characters." "Looks at school and life more realistically than do most books for teenagers." "You ask yourself if this could really happen."

Elliott, David. *Listen to the Silence*.

A fourteen-year-old struggles to survive in a mental institution where he is placed because no one really wants him. "Makes you feel the frustrations and sorrows of an unwanted child."

Godey, John. *The Taking of Pelham One Two Three*.

Gunmen hijack a subway in New York City and hold the passengers for ransom. "The excitement and tension build up as you read along."

Griffin, John Howard. *Black Like Me*.

Griffin, a White man, blackens his skin and travels through the South as a Negro. "It was painful to read how humans can be so inhumane to other men." "Excellent." "Astonishing."

Hano, Arnold. *Roberto Clemente: Batting King*.

A story of the struggles of the great National League batting star who died while on a mission of mercy. "It is more than just a life story, it told how he felt about others."

Harris, Marilyn. *Hatter Fox.*

A shocking story of a rebellious Indian girl and the young doctor who tries to help. "The book was great. I haven't read a book of this size in two nights ever before." "Once you start reading you can't stop." "We cannot live for ourselves alone."

Hesse, Hermann. *Demian.*

A forceful Demian influences his friend Sinclair in a philosophical struggle for individualism. "Fascinating book." "Delves into the Taoist philosophy of the balance between good and evil." "Teaches you a lot about life." "A difficult book to read but it was fun to figure out."

Koenig, Laird. *The Little Girl Who Lives Down the Lane.*

The thirteen-year-old "little" girl meets Mario who becomes devoted to her and keeps her secret. "Fascinating." "Unusual." "One of the best." "Rynn did not value life enough to care if others live or die." "I could never say enough good things about this book."

Samuels, Gertrude. *Run, Shelly, Run!*

A sixteen-year-old runs from foster homes and detention centers in her attempt to discover identity, self-respect, and freedom. Based on truth, this novel is powerful and compassionate. "A good account of how young people can become victims of circumstance." "Fantastic book." "I'd recommend it to any teenage boy or girl."

Stein, Sol. *The Magician.*

A high school senior and an attorney perform some magic of their own and the reader is left to ponder over the puzzling question of justice. "Suspenseful, started reading and did not want to stop." "Ending was ironic and surprising." "Never a boring moment."

Thompson, Thomas. *Richie.*

A true story about a boy who becomes a drug addict, drifts away from his family, and meets a tragic end. "A very exciting book." "Very interesting." "Hard to put down." "Recommend for anyone."

Tolkien, J.R.R. *The Hobbit.*

The author creates delightful people smaller than dwarfs, not as fierce as goblins, much like elves, but very down to earth and places them in a fantasy land called Middle Earth. "Good book, very out of the ordinary." "Truly a unique book." "Refreshing." "Most outstanding book I have ever read." "A fairy tale for grown-ups."

Trumbo, Dalton. *Johnny Got His Gun.*

A World War I veteran reminisces in his hospital bed contemplating his future and the future of the world. ''Best book I've picked up all year.'' ''Excellent and touching.'' ''Shocking fiction.'' ''To wake people out of their apathetic hibernation.''

Vonnegut, Kurt, Jr. *Cat's Cradle.*

A social satire and fantasy about the end of the world. ''Will technology go too far and kill us all?'' ''Surrealistic style.''

Vonnegut, Kurt, Jr. *Slaughterhouse Five.*

A prisoner of war witnesses the fire bombing of Dresden and survives to tell the tale, sees into the future and relives the past. ''This was one of the most mind-boggling books I have ever read.''

Wersba, Barbara. *Run Softly, Go Fast.*

A seventeen-year-old drifts away from his father and returns too late to close the gap. ''A book which really makes you think.'' ''I liked the book because David talked about his inner feelings.''

Woiwode, L. *What I'm Going to Do, I Think.*

Newlyweds struggle to adjust to each other and overcome the frustrations of the past. ''This book is a good example of how an author should involve his reader.''

Read and Rock—A Special Kind of Reading Center

by Ann B. Madison

The entrance to our school was grim and not at all inviting. We wanted to make it an appealing place that would tell children that we were involved in things that interested them. Because reading is the nucleus of our curriculum, we also wanted to create an atmosphere that would let our students know that we are a reading society and that reading at our school is exciting.

We built a center in the school's front hall that would be seen by everyone who entered. It had a prefabricated fireplace, an oval braided rug, several rocking chairs, small stools, cushions, and a bookshelf holding comic books about Spiderman, paperbacks about Snoopy, the comic section from Sunday's paper, and books with riddles, magic tricks, and the answers to the hundreds of questions children ask about their world. There were cereal boxes holding an enormous number of fun things to read, magazines, and books filled with easily duplicated arts and crafts projects. The center, called Read and Rock, held all of the fun kinds of things to read that are not generally found in media centers or the average classroom.

It was a place to visit between, during, before, and after classes— anytime someone felt like reading and rocking. It was a moderately popular place, but materials were quickly exhausted and expensive to substitute or replace on our limited budget, so we decided to ask the children to write short stories, books, poetry, or plays on interesting subjects and place them in the center.

Stories trickled in for a week or so, then a group of our lowest achievers in reading decided to pool their efforts and write a book describing their classroom experience in making homemade modeling clay. The story was recorded by the teacher, typed, bound in book form, and illustrated by its authors. The reading teacher placed the students' book on the shelf in the center, then it was read over the public address system for everyone to hear. These children had received very little recognition, at least of a positive nature, for any of their work, and now their efforts had been shared with their classmates.

Signs were also posted bearing the names of other contributors of materials and promoting their works. One sign read, "What's the most embarrassing thing that ever happened to you? Come to Read and Rock and read what happened to Charlie Burns in his book entitled 'Oh No! Not Me!'" Another sign posted on a mirror read, "Mirror, mirror on the wall, who is the meanest dog of them all? Come to Read and Rock and read the story called 'Mean Dog' by Beverly King."

By the next day there was an undercurrent of excitement and a heightened curiosity in Read and Rock. Children were heard saying to each other, "Wonder how you get to have your name on the speaker?" and "I'm gonna write a book about Godzilla."

From then on, authors and illustrators appeared in ever increasing numbers. Within three weeks, 75 books had been written, illustrated, and donated. These books became the most popular reading material in the school.

The ego-building self-confidence that came with authorship and recognition led to the development of our Happy Gram Delivery. Happy Grams are miniature telegrams that read: They are delivered in a large envelope to children who contribute their works to Read and Rock, and they are inscribed with the message:

HAPPY GRAM

We have recently discovered something new and exciting about your child and would like to share it with you.

_____

_____

_____

To you:

　　　　Happy Gram

You have been discovered and we are HAPPY about it! Your carrier for today is

Children generally try to please their teachers, peers, and parents, so they are eager to take these messages home to share with their families.

Assistance in writing stories is provided by the teacher if requested. However, stories are written in the child's language and include all of the characteristics of the particular dialect and syntactic language pattern of the author. If a child chooses to submit his composition, it is not edited for errors in spelling, grammar, or sequence of events.

The students are now producing from eight to fifteen books per day. One class has organized a group of students to do reviews of the books donated to Read and Rock. A child from the group gives a daily review over the public address system to motivate others to look for particular books of interest when they visit the center.

In the future, we plan to form publishing committees composed of the students who have been identified as gifted and talented in the area of language arts to assist the young authors who find it difficult to compose a story alone. The committees will transcribe stories dictated to the recorder, type, and bind books.

Our Read and Rock activities have helped us point out to all our students the importance of writing legibly; of designing attractive, eye-catching book covers; and of expressing ideas clearly. Insight into career awareness has been brought into the curriculum as the children experience firsthand the joys and frustrations of authors and illustrators. An opportunity for role playing has been provided as children are free to characterize themselves during the creation of stories, poems, and plays.

Teachers have found that students' books are excellent tools for diagnosing instructional needs in the communication skills areas.

Getting Kids Into Books:
The Importance of
Individualized Reading

by Terry C. Ley

Several years ago, someone told me that two-thirds of our nation's population had read its last book by age eighteen. While I've never run across that statistic again, I've worked with adolescents long enough to believe that it's true. And other figures have come rushing. Surveys by the National Opinion Research Center show that: (1) citizens of the United States read fewer books than citizens of Great Britain, France, Germany, Holland, Switzerland, and the Scandinavian countries; (2) approximately 10 percent of our population reads approximately 80 percent of the books read; (3) about half the adult population of the U.S. has never read a book all the way through; (4) less than one out of five adults could name a book they would like to read.

Part of what these figures reflect is our failure to prepare students to find pleasure in reading. They indict the practices in our schools—and particularly our high schools, and many of our English classrooms—that do little to encourage lifetime reading habits, and in fact often inhibit the pleasure from which such habits might develop. Outside of an environment in which reading (often dull and difficult) is required, students do as little of it as possible. Indeed, when most of them graduate, they leave the reading of books behind with other tasks that they see little use for, and too often associate with pain: writing themes and research papers, delivering persuasive four-minute speeches, underlining subjects once and predicates twice.

Reminded almost daily of our failure to prepare students to cope with the print media, confused by legions of objectives and ranks of skills and subskills, frustrated by our own limited knowledge of reading instruction, we too often settle for observed behavior which tells us that students can detect an author's purpose—and neglect our responsibility to help young people *want* to read, to help them discover or rediscover the joy and the insight which unread pages promise. We settle for short-term cognitive goals and lose sight of our opportunities as significant adults to encourage positive attitudes and habits in young people that they will take with them and use when they leave school.

Research and informal observation give us information about reading and adolescents which can assist teachers seeking ways to encourage both skill development and lifetime reading habits in their students: (1) *Students coming into our classrooms represent a wide range of reading ability.* A teacher working with a heterogeneous tenth-grade class, for instance, can expect to deal with a ten-year range of reading ability. The poorest readers may struggle to comprehend (having fifth-grade readability levels) while the best readers may read college-level materials easily and well. (2) *Students bring different sets of capabilities and experiences to their reading*—sets defined by socioeconomic environments, physical and mental characteristics, and educational backgrounds. Motivation and ability to reach one's potential as a reader are greatly affected by the unique set which each student possesses. (3) *Students have varied interests which may affect their willingness to read.* Teachers should be aware that reading interests of adolescents are likely to be closely related to developmental tasks which they must cope with as they pass from childhood to adulthood. According to G. Robert Carlsen (*Books and the Teenage Reader,* Bantam), today's adolescents, like preceding generations of adolescents, appear to be extremely interested in (a) discovering their respective sex roles in our culture, (b) developing new relationships with people their own age, (c) achieving an easy relationship with members of the opposite sex, (d) accepting their physical bodies, (e) changing their relationships with their parents, (f) working for pay, (g) finding a vocation, and (h) becoming aware of their value patterns. Note that this list is neither sequential nor cumulative. Teachers must expect their students to be at various stages of development and must realize that one student may not yet have felt the nudge of the very task which keeps another student awake at night and distracted throughout the next day's discussion of *A Separate Peace*.

Bookshelves are filled with works which speak to these tasks, many of them written by authors sensitive to the benefits which adolescents can derive from observing others who deal realistically with problems similar to their own. Unfortunately, coping with their own personal problems demands so much of adolescents' time and energy that they seldom get around to checking out and reading any of those books. Athletics, part-time jobs, and group activities with peers are attractive because they offer adolescents opportunities to achieve bits of independence which, they hope, will soon resolve themselves into adulthood. Even students who have been avid readers as children frequently sacrifice recreational reading during their junior high and senior high years because more immediate personal concerns claim their interest and time.

While these facts and observations are not new to most experienced teachers, they do have special implications which teachers of English in secondary schools may wish to consider. Far too many teachers rely heavily upon in-common reading experiences as the major vehicle for communicating what English and reading have to offer. They invest a major proportion of literature/reading instructional time in consideration of common readings of classic proportion—expecting 30 students to read the same piece of literature at the same time.

In-common reading experiences, if wisely planned and carefully directed, are valuable for teaching literature/reading skills, of course. They become tools for teachers who wish to assist groups of young people to become independent readers. However, students whose reading experiences are selected almost exclusively by the teacher—often from a book which at least half the class cannot read independently and which may offer content of marginal interest to a minority of class members—may begin to associate even the reading of imaginative literature with failure, pain, duty—anything but pleasure. It is ironic and sad that so many teachers who feel it their duty to tour the anthology and its outlying paperbacks with their students (and who may do so with considerable flair) often work very hard to prepare students for other trips, trips those students will choose not to take.

A personal dimension within secondary school literature/reading programs seems imperative. Such a dimension should allow for the wide range of reading abilities found in any classroom; it should recognize the diversity and the continually shifting focus of adolescents' needs and interests; and it should provide generous amounts of class time for personal reading and appropriate follow-up activities. Students should be allowed to select materials which they can read and which interest them. They should be encouraged to read at a comfortable pace in a quiet environment, surrounded by a variety of appealing materials and a room full of peers who are enjoying the same privileges. Follow-up or feedback requirements should allow students to select activities which they are comfortable with, but which will also demand the thoughtful consideration of literary experiences they have selected for themselves. Individualized reading programs of this sort are probably most successful when blocks of time are consciously set aside by individual teachers or better yet, by entire English staffs as they are developing curriculum.

Free-reading-every-Friday may have many of the desirable characteristics of a personal reading dimension, but because it does not provide consecutive days for reading the same book, students often lose interest (or lose the book) before they have finished it. A student reading three chapters of a book each Friday for five weeks is probably less likely to demonstrate keen comprehension of the book than a student allowed to read the entire book during five consecutive class periods.

Students are aware of the need for individualizing and personalizing the literature/reading program and are generally anxious to contribute to the success of that dimension. Asked what a teacher of theirs had done or could do to interest them in reading, one thousand students at Nathaniel Hawthorne Middle School, Bayside, New York offered these responses, among others: Let us choose our own books. Suggest names of interesting stories. Let us read along with taped stories. Assign creative projects instead of book reports. Let us read comic books, magazines, and newspapers. Take us to the school library. Have a classroom library. Bring appropriate book clubs to the attention of students. Prepare teacher and/or student annotated book lists. Let us read at our own pace. (Donna Brutton, ''How to Develop and Maintain Student interest in Reading,'' *English Journal,* November 1974.)

A self-selection/self-pacing personal reading dimension—commonly referred to as Directed Individualized Reading (DIR) or simply as Individualized Reading—is a response to students' requests and to present knowledge of reading, psychology, and adolescent interests. Though DIR has taken many forms in schools, essentially those forms are variations on a very simple theme: Students select material which they wish to read, devote consecutive English class periods to reading, and select a method for communicating to others their impressions of what they have read.

The value of DIR programs can be determined in several ways. The individual teacher may be impressed by the quantity of reading accomplished during DIR units—an indication of the amount of reading practice provided by the freedom to read which DIR implies. One teacher found that the 45 students in his two ninth-grade English classes read 26,499 pages during their three-week unit, an average of nearly 600 pages per reader. If the same students had each read 40 pages a week in a literature anthology, they would have completed 5400 pages—only one-fifth as much.

More significant than the number of pages read, however, is the variety of materials selected and completed, a variety which emphasizes the diversity of needs, interests, and reading abilities present in any class. Tim, a member of one of the ninth-grade classes referred to above, selected and read *The Agony and the Ecstasy* (Stone), *The Jungle* (Sinclair), and *Anthem* (Rand) during a three-week unit. Gary read *I Am Third* (Sayers) and *The Martian Chronciles* (Bradbury). Julia read *Karen* (Killilea) and *Flowers for Algernon* (Keyes). Liz completed only one book, *The Nun's Story* (Hulme). Lisa, one of the brightest girls in the ninth grade but not ordinarily an avid reader, read seven books: *Red Sky at Morning* (Bradford), *Tell Me that You Love Me, Junie Moon* (Kellogg), *Just Dial a Number* (Maxwell), *Good*

Morning, Miss Dove (Paton), *An American Girl* (Dizenzo), *Wedding Song* (Crane), and *1984* (Orwell).

That individualized reading programs are instructional and lead to positive attitudes toward reading was clearly established by research conducted by Bruce C. Appleby ("Individualized Reading as Environment for the Literary Experience," in *The Creative Teacher*, ed. by William Evans, Bantam). He compared differences which existed among three groups: 65 high school seniors at four different ability levels enrolled in a one-semester individualized reading course; 65 seniors at four different ability levels who had wanted to take the individualized reading course but who were not taking it; and 65 seniors at four different ability levels who were taking a required, traditional literature course.

Appleby discovered that individualized reading "accomplishes the objectives of a literature program as well as, if not better than, other types of literature instruction." No differences favored the control groups over the individualized reading group. Perhaps most important, students who had been enrolled in individualized reading showed more positive attitudes toward fiction and more satisfaction with literary experience than did those in the control groups. Such positive attitudes and satisfactions are, of course, fundamental to establishing the habit of lifetime personal reading.

How to Set Up and Evaluate a DIR Program

by Terry C. Ley

Theodore Weesner introduced Alex Houseman to me in his novel *The Car Thief* several years ago, and I recommend that you get to know him. Should you read his story, you will find that several of your own students bear a resemblance to Alex—not because they look like him or cut your classes or steal cars, but because, left to their own devices as they are, they are growing up bent and lonely and joyless, with few human models whose traits they care to emulate.

As an English teacher I am especially concerned with the forces which shape our young people as they emerge into adulthood. I know that both real and vicarious experiences have their influences on our students, and I am certain that reading can provide valuable vicarious experiences for them and can thus assist their growth. I consider it one of my greatest professional challenges to find reading matter of probable value to my students and to share it with them, as I'm sure most English teachers do.

But many students, like Alex, do not read even if they are skilled readers. They do not have or do not take the time to examine the lives of Anne Frank or Holden Caulfield or Francie Nolan or Randle McMurphy or Scout Finch—and are worse for lost opportunities to measure themselves and the directions of their lives against worthy models. We must give them not only the skills for reading, but also the time to do it—and the will.

Alex could read but had done little of it. Then, while institutionalized following his theft of a Buick Riviera, he has nothing but time and a stack of donated books—a promising combination, I think. Alex selects his first book and responds to his reading in a manner we would like to duplicate repeatedly for our students—and ourselves. I felt great hope for Alex as I read *The Car Thief*. His brief experience with meaningful reading did remain strong in his memory, but reading did not become a permanent habit for him within the few months his story covers. I should have known! After all these years, it is clear to me that lifetime reading habits probably grow out of repeated experience such as Alex's—and the message I would like to write large is that we must not leave such opportunities for our students to chance. We must assume responsibilities for teaching reading skills to our students as long as they are with us in our schools; as they develop independence as readers, we must provide genuine opportunities for personal reading in our classrooms, then step aside and let them read.

Directed Individualized Reading (DIR) does just that. Students are allowed to select books *they* want to read, given uninterrupted time to do the reading, and provided a format for feedback and evaluation. Coupled with what I consider an essential component—individualized teacher/student conferences—the program also affords teachers an excellent opportunity to assess the interests and skill levels in their classrooms.

Three-week blocks set aside for DIR each semester provide time for students with average reading abilities to read two or three books during each unit. After getting to know a class and the individuals in it, and particularly if a class contains many students who read poorly, you may decide that two weeks are as long as they will be able to sustain interest in DIR, and plan accordingly. Elective courses in DIR, nine to eighteen weeks long, are extremely popular when they are well taught and when the curriculum allows students to become familiar with the principles of DIR before they take part in it.

FINDING BOOKS FOR STUDENTS SELECTION

So long as a wide range of reading materials is available, students with diverse reading abilities can find success and pleasure in DIR. Students may select long or short pieces of prose or poetry to read in class and outside of class. Their reading choices may be directly or indirectly influenced ("directed") by you, the teacher. Since availability is a major factor influencing choice of reading materials, you should attempt to surround students with high-interest materials in the classroom and to make their use of the school library desirable and convenient. The teacher without a classroom collection of books and magazines can borrow materials from the school library for classroom use during DIR, or can ask students to share materials from their personal collections. Frequent "selling" sessions may provide direction for some readers, as may attractive displays of popular books or books sharing themes related to developmental tasks and current interests (e.g., books and articles about drugs or teenage marriage). Book lists—always annotated—may be offered but should never limit students' reading choices.

Your most valuable opportunity for directing students toward a pleasant reading experience comes when you can talk personally to each of them, particularly during book conferences which may become a major aspect of DIR. During those conversations you may make recommendations based on what you have discovered about the student's response to his or her current reading, present hobbies or interests, and reading ability. Clues drawn from conversation may lead you to suggest reading related to a variety of themes, or you may sense that the student is prepared to move vertically within an area of interest which he or she has pursued for some time—that is, to read a more complex book about war or horses or basketball than the one just finished. Questionnaires may also be used to poll reading interests and thus to assist you in your role as advisor. Some teachers use book club order blanks as a means of gathering information about student interests. Students pretend they have $5.00 to spend on current paperback offerings; they read the annotations, fill out the order blank, and help tally the results. Whenever money is available, the teachers order the four or five books most often requested by their students.

Your value as an advisor increases as you become better acquainted with materials which interest your students and with their responses to those materials. If you are not familiar with several hundred titles, you are likely to find professionally prepared annotated book lists—usually organized according to themes or subjects—extremely helpful. Among the most useful book lists for secondary school teachers are G. Robert Carlsen's *Books and the Teen-age Reader* (Bantam), Virginia Reid's *Reading Ladders for Human Relations* (Ace), Marian E. White's *High Interest—Easy Reading for Junior and Senior High School Students* (Scholastic), Betty M. Owen's *Smorgasbord of Books* (Scholastic), and two NCTE book lists, Jerry L. Walker's *Your Reading* (junior high school) and Kenneth L. Donelson's *Books for You* (senior high school). Materials for teachers which accompany each month's book club brochures from Scholastic and Xerox are also valuable.

SETTING UP THE PROGRAM

Each day's initial activities should be designed to build interest in reading certain books and to provide opportunities for sharing responses to completed books. You might begin by sharing with the class something that you have read, or by "selling" two or three books for which you think there's a market. You may ask that if anyone has finished a book since the last class meeting, they tell something about the book which might interest the class. Those who decide to share their responses with the class through one of several alternative projects may also do so at the beginning of the period. In addition, a number of brief lessons might be interspersed to introduce or review skills or concepts related to pleasure reading. Such lessons could include frequent timed readings, using whatever materials students are currently reading; instruction in using an index card as a pacer; techniques for scanning books when selecting reading materials; and hints on caring for books. Information about book publishing—particularly paperback production—may also interest DIR groups. No more than ten minutes should be devoted to introductory activities.

Since personal reading is the center of all activity in DIR, the majority of each class period ought to be spent in quiet reading. During any given period, portions of the class may (1) read, (2) have conferences with the teacher, (3) prepare for conferences or work on alternate projects, or (4) select something to read. Students should be encouraged to continue their reading between class periods and taught how to pace themselves through a book. However, expectations for out-of-class reading will vary with the class and the individuals in it; students who find the right books are likely to continue their reading between classes without the pressure of an assignment.

EVALUATING A DIR PROGRAM

Though some relatively objective methods of evaluating and grading were developed early in the evolution of DIR—many of them based on point systems—those who have worked with it for many years have turned to a more subjective approach. Early methods rated student performance on their writing, their conferences, or their feedback projects. Those ratings were then greatly influenced by the difficulty and the length of the books read. However, students who read slowly or poorly or reluctantly are often unduly penalized by such point systems, even in homogeneous classes. Subjective evaluation and grading methods will undoubtedly be most appropriate for DIR; however, teachers should explain those methods before students start their reading.

A simple one-page hand-out can provide the basis for initial discussion of objectives, use of class time, and the bases for grading. The following variables might be listed by a teacher who wishes to evaluate DIR subjectively: quantity read; challenge offered to the individual student by the materials read; the maturity of any required written work; the quality of book conferences the student has with the teacher, or of other projects which the student completes; and the student's use of class time for DIR activity.

Quantity: Obviously, reading two relatively short, simple books during DIR may represent as much effort for one student as reading considerably more books does for another reader. Though you may wish to keep a record of the total number of pages each student reads, that number must be but one of several evaluative measures. Goals, especially where grades are concerned, probably should not be expressed in numbers of pages, though some individual students may be partially motivated by a mounting number of pages read. It is important, of course, that the students and the teacher keep careful accounts of readings and conferences or projects completed.

Challenge: The degree of challenge offered by a student's reading choices is relative to a number of factors, of course, but perhaps none is so important as a student's ability to read. Scores on standardized or informal reading tests and informal observation throughout the course will help you assess the challenge factor for your DIR students.

Written work: As evidence of their consideration of a book they have just finished reading, students might be asked to complete a four-by-six-inch card and submit it the day before they have a conference or at the time of the conference. Ask for information on the card which encourages the students to evaluate certain aspects of their recent reading experience. If a student submits his or her card with the book a day before the conference is scheduled, you can use the card to prepare for the conference, drawing from it matters which you hope to discuss with the student.

In addition to bibliographic information, the student may be asked to include a brief plot summary or annotation, and opinions or reactions to the book. Concepts emphasized in discussion of previous in-common, reading experiences may serve as the basis for any analytic comments required. (For instance, students who have recently examined the relationship of subplots to the major plot in conjunction with an in-common reading of a novel, might be asked to apply this analysis to novels they choose to read during DIR.) It often helps if you mark the card to guide you during the conference, establishing beforehand at least a question or two that you would like to discuss.

Conference: The student-teacher conference—ten to fifteen minutes in length—is a most desirable means of assessing a student's insight into longer works that she or he has read. The conference should be informal, conversational, and distinctly nonthreatening. While the student may be asked to prepare for the conference by writing a card, the teacher must prepare by becoming acquainted with the book, perhaps by skimming it, and examining the student's card for appropriate matters to discuss.

Not all questions that one might ask about a literary experience are equally challenging, of course, and teachers who wish to use conferences as informal diagnostic tools must become skillful in their selection of such questions. Some readers are able to draw inferences from or evaluate what they read quite easily, while others must struggle for even literal comprehension. Early conferences should be used to establish at what level of reading comprehension a student operates comfortably; later conferences should encourage the student to build upward from that point. During a typical conference, student and teacher might discuss topics suggested by these general quetions: Why did you choose to read this book? Who tells the story? What are two or three of the main problems the major character faces? How does he or she solve those problems? Which of the characters do you admire? What was your favorite part of the story? Are any of the characters like someone you know? Do you think this story would make a good movie? How would the movie probably differ from the book? Did you have trouble understanding any part of the story? Could you figure out the story's ending in advance? Were you satisfied with the ending when you got it? Have you ever read a story similar to this one? Would you like to read another one like it sometime?

Conversations with students about their responses to what they have read are excellent sources of information for teachers alert to the need for informal diagnosis of students'—and whole classes'—reading strengths and weaknesses. The teacher who has recently emphasized the relationship of major plot and subplots in a specific novel should welcome an opportunity to evaluate the students' ability to apply their understanding to personal reading. One junior high reading teacher I know asks each student to select from the book one or two paragraphs that contain vivid imagery, or that tell about an exciting event, and to read the passage aloud to her during the conference. She listens with an ear for diagnosis and frequently asks students a question or two related to their comprehension of the passage. Used wisely, the book conference yields information helpful not only in understanding the personalities and the reading capabilities of individual students, but also in assessing the reading needs of groups or entire classes, and in planning for subsequent instruction.

Unfortunately, teachers often neglect the conference component because it requires preparation time and a good deal of skill and energy. Teachers who insist upon having conferences each time they teach DIR discover that these conferences become easier to prepare for as one grows increasingly familiar with literally hundreds of books which the students read over a period of years. Many of these teachers save the most useful cards submitted by their students and refer to them often. They become adept at skimming—sometimes because they are pressed for time and sometimes because they realize the material at hand does not require thorough reading for their present purposes. They gain skill in asking productive questions in a nonthreatening manner. And they find personal pleasure in talking informally with their students, discovering numerous professional benefits as a result.

Alternative Feedback Projects: In addition to the conference—or as a substitute for it—you may want to suggest other approaches for obtaining student feedback on books read. These can include any number of techniques: constructing collages; drawing illustrations, posters, or book jackets; writing back-cover blurbs; assuming the identity of a character in the book and writing a letter to another character; taping or filming a commercial for the book or an oral interpretation of portions of the text which substantiate an opinion; dramatizing a part of the book.

THE BENEFITS OF DIR

Preparing young people for both independence and pleasure as they come in contact with the print media is an objective formidable enough to warrant serious efforts by teachers at all grade levels and in all content areas, of course. Secondary school English teachers can make a special contribution to this effort by providing precious time for those students to get sustained practice, while reading materials that appeal to them and that they are capable of handling. Conferences allow teachers to give individual attention to each student's responses to her or his reading and, in doing so, to observe, probe, and diagnose reading capability, with an eye to future instruction. They also provide students with valuable opportunities to hone their perceptions and sharpen their conversation skills.

Above all, DIR encourages continued interest in personal reading as a natural and rewarding activity. It helps young people to see that reading can be an enjoyable and profitable experience as well as an opportunity for informal exchange with others—including, in this case, a student and a teacher.

PART
IV

NONPRINT

Introduction

Nonprint production used as a motivator to entice students to read is a widespread practice. Teachers and library media specialists, in attempting to discover an alternative or nontraditional approach to reading, have often found that students are captivated by nonprint production and have an almost innate talent for both operation of the equipment and production of the nonprint item.

Nonprint, as defined by the editors of this compilation, means *any* type of materials other than the conventional book format. Others have chosen *nonbook* to stand for the opposite of book or *media* to describe this area; however, *nonprint* appears to be more representative of this field.

Each of the articles in this section deals with some aspect of nonprint. David Barber-Smith and Susan Smith Reilly in "Use Media to Motivate Reading" explore a variety of techniques they have found to be successful in working with learning disabled students. Their program "has produced high-interest audiovisual materials with subject content not available in textbooks written at low reading levels." Wilber S. Slawson in "Making Homemade Filmstrips" explains how students can create an unusual type of filmstrip using paper and an opaque projector. Resource materials which the students must read and transfer into picture and written format form this instructional experience. "Turning Kids On to Print" by James L. Thomas contends that "tuned out" children can be "turned on" with nonprint productions. In this article the author maintains that this type of production can be used as a catalyst to promote the reluctant reader to read. In "If I Read This Book . . . Do I Have to Write a Book Report?" Carolyn Paine presents a number of alternatives to standard book reporting, such as reporting with pictures and a quilt that spreads the word.

Finally, two articles propose the use of games as a tool in motivating children to read. Karen Steiner in "Child's Play: Games to Teach Reading" maintains that "Games and simulations are excellent tools for stimulating student motivation," especially in reading skill development. George Canney in "Commercial Games—Made Relevant for Reading" discusses why and how to go about integrating reading games into the curriculum. The author also lists the materials—title, publisher, and approximate cost—to start the game reading approach.

Use Media to Motivate Reading

by David Barber-Smith
and Susan Smith Reilly

How can a teacher motivate a 16-year-old student to read when that student has a third-year reading level? This problem provides subject matter for many a teacher's and media specialist's nightmares.

Learning disability is a condition recognized in school-aged children where peripheral vision and hearing are normal, intelligence is average, and there has been adequate cultural opportunity to learn, but academic functioning is two or more years behind the expectation of academic experts. This lag is attributed to minimal brain dysfunction including central nervous system processing deficits, dyslexia, and perceptual motor difficulties.

Although learning disabled children have average intelligence or above, they function academically at levels significantly below their potential. Reading presents a major problem to a majority of these students. This reading disability severely hampers their efforts to learn other subjects. As they encounter continual academic failure, they often withdraw from classroom exercises and suffer from declining self-esteem. Often children with learning disabilities—especially older children—are so discouraged with the educational process that motivation to participate in classroom activities becomes a major issue before learning can begin.

For the past two years the audiovisual program at Wordsworth Academy has experienced success using media to encourage student motivation for reading. Our program has produced high-interest audiovisual materials with subject content not available in textbooks written at low reading levels. These materials were produced through student productions using photography, film, and television.

In the class productions involving photography, students created their own stories orally. The teachers transcribed these stories onto paper. The media specialist worked with the students to illustrate the stories with photographs. The story and accompanying photographs were organized with a layout into a book format. The books were photocopied and used as reading material in the classroom. A high level of enthusiasm and student involvement was achieved and maintained throughout the project. The books were widely read by students from other classes as well as by the participants themselves.

With these books, reading was required primarily with the completed product. In film and television productions, however, the students needed to read throughout the process of preparing scripts for productions. One science class decided to produce a film as part of a unit on famous historical scientists. They selected, as a setting, a modern-day convention of great minds where famous people from the past would gather to discuss their work. Each of the students in the class chose a particular scientist to portray. They then researched that scientist's life and summarized it in an auto-biographical narrative style. This became part of the film's script. The students also met in groups of two, where they created conversations between scientists.

The class members spent a considerable amount of time reading and rehearsing their narrations and conversations. Since they were interested in creating a quality production, they were motivated to spend time studying their scripts. By the time the filming and recording took place, the class was well prepared. The teacher felt that their motivation to read while engaged in this project was significantly greater than they had shown in any other reading activity during the year.

This class also created a playbill that was distributed when the film was shown to the other classes in the school. This consisted of a brief outline of the plot and biographical sketches of each of the student actors.

Television is a medium to which children are quite attuned. They are excited at the opportunity to be both behind and in front of the camera. We have found that children are motivated to work hard at reading involved in the television production process.

One production that helped motivate reading, initiated by a teacher working with the media specialist, was a student newscast. For this show, each member of the class played a specific role on the news team—anchor, sports reporter, weather forecaster, on-the-scene reporter. Each then wrote his or her own story, based on news both within and outside the school. The class spent an entire week reading and rehearsing its news stories. Finally the program was videotaped and replayed to their entire unit on Friday.

These projects involving photography, film, and television show that nonprint media can help motivate reading with the learning disabled child, while encouraging active participation from all students. They allow students to create their own reading material, which is generally more relevant to them than the material they normally encounter in the classroom.

If students discover that they can improve their reading, even slightly, through participation in media productions, they may feel more motivated to read in other instances. If students experience some success in an academic area that was previously frustrating and discouraging, they are likely to feel an increase in self-esteem. This increase often translates into greater efforts in the classroom, both academically and socially.

Creativity is another issue involved in media projects. Allowing students freedom to determine what subject to explore, which medium to use, and what their reading material will be encourages creative expression. Participation in the creative process cannot help but increase motivation and enthusiasm within the classroom.

Making Homemade Filmstrips

by Wilber S. Slawson

Many times successful involvement of children in the main instructional block is hampered by a less than successful lead-in experience. It is within this context that the following ideas are proposed, for the filmstrip is meant to be an initiatory experience to future study of the subject material being emphasized. It could also serve as a culminating experience. The ideas presented are time consuming so it is up to the teacher to establish the point at which there might be diminishing returns. By the same token, extended periods of time might very well be warranted. The idea is developed around science phenomena but it should be evident that the idea is equally useful in other areas as well.

Method: The goal is to create a filmstrip that illustrates future involvement in the instructional program. The filmstrip is student made and is characterized by a series of individual pieces of regular writing paper taped together and fed through an opaque projector. Since students are approaching the learning experience without benefit of previous organized instruction, resource material must be available to aid in helping them individually create "frames" for the filmstrip. Obviously, perfection is not sought at this point and students should be encouraged to respond to the directions on the card without fear of reprisal.

Picture, if you will, 30 students busily engaged in responding to 30 sets of directions on 30 cards, and you begin to get the picture. To obtain a degree of uniformity the students can be guided in such things as putting the paper in the same manner when responding (longest part horizontal is suggested), putting the number of their direction card in one corner of the frame (insures proper sequencing of finished product), and putting their name on the frame (gives them a vested interest in the final product). Students should further be encouraged to be creative and have fun in the process of designing their responses.

As students will finish at differing times, it is wise to have extending group types of activities to channel them into as they complete their individual involvement in making the filmstrip. Some suggestions are to assign two or three children the responsibility of actually putting the filmstrip together in the proper sequence and being the technicians in running the final product through the opaque projector. Another extending activity could be to assign a group of students the task of creating a song about simple machines, a poem about simple machines, a skit about simple machines, a bulletin board (or some type of pictorial presentation on the board, or a mural), developing and/or playing some kind of card game using ideas related to simple machines.

Instead of just one initiatory activity of the filmstrip we now have many initiatory activities that have been *student created* and can be used from that point on in various ways within the instructional setting. In addition to the motivational aspects of the activity, there are other more subtle advantages. For example, it can have a diagnostic purpose in terms of individuals because the materials were student made. Also the students have a vested interest in the instructional materials because they made them. Instructional materials have been developed plus common references experienced for future use in the subject matter involvement and the development of them has been fun for students. There have also been social opportunities for students because of the group involvement.

Materials Needed: paper, scotch tape, marking pens, opaque projector, old file folders (to be cut up), assortment of materials to build with, resource materials.

Sample Cards for Filmstrip (directions put on 3 x 5 cards): These are distributed one per child.

1. Design a title page for the filmstrip. *Be creative.*
2. Define the words *simple machine* and write it on your paper.
3. List and *draw* an example of the six simple machines on your paper.
4. Draw a picture of an inclined plane and label the following: length of the plane, height of the plane.
5. Copy this diagram on your paper:

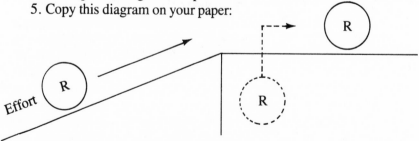

6. Write these questions on your paper:
   1. Does an inclined plane decrease the amount of effort needed to overcome the resistance?
   2. Does it take longer to do work if you use an inclined plane?
   3. Is the effort applied through a greater distance using an inclined plane?

So the questions continue until you have enough direction cards for everyone and have basically covered the material included in the experience.

PUTTING THE FILMSTRIP TOGETHER

The main thing is to get the papers in sequence, which is easily accomplished because of the numbers transferred from the direction cards.

Composing a Song:

Old Doc Slawson
(sung to the tune of Old MacDonald)

Old Doc Slawson had machines,
    Simple though they be.
Many kinds did he possess;
    Sing along and see.
With a lever, lever here
    and a lever, lever there
Here a lever, there a lever;
    Everywhere a lever, lever;
Old Doc Slawson had machines,
    Simple though *he* be!

Of course, other machines would represent additional verses.

Composing a Poem: Requires the same type of application as composing a song but it's easier since it doesn't have to be put to music.

L is for lever, now let's be clever
    a stick and a stone plus proper position
makes your work much easier
    with less work for the physician!
P is for pulley . . .

Preparing a Skit: Potential roles for students could be Louie Lever, Fanny Force, Esther Effort, Frankie Fulcrum, and Robert Resistance Arm, Evelyn Effort Arm, and the various relationships existing between these forces represent possibilities for the script for the play.

A Pictorial Presentation:

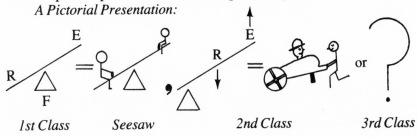

1st Class   *Seesaw*   *2nd Class*   *3rd Class*

Playing Cards: A possibility would be to cut appropriate sized cards from old file folders and design them in a manner to match up into pairs. For example, some cards have the word *lever* and some the word *pulley,* and so forth, while other cards have pictures representing examples of the machines. A pair then becomes a lever card plus a card with a picture of a lever on it. These would be fine to play concentration, rummy or any other game that depends on pairing to play. An additional card with the picture of an old maid makes the deck appropriate to play old maid.

Any of the instructional materials developed in the initiatory activity can be used in various ways within the later teaching strategies for actually teaching understanding of the subject matter material. The possibilities are limitless.

Turning Kids On to Print

by James L. Thomas

From my years of experience as a secondary and an elementary media librarian, I have become convinced that "tuned out" children can be "turned on" with media. While this in itself appears to be a worthy goal, I think that media is used to best advantage when it serves as a catalyst to return children willingly to the world of print.

While serving as librarian at a private military academy for high school aged boys, my background in English and speech made me the only candidate for teaching a course in public speaking. The postgraduates for whom the course had been planned were young men who had had academic difficulties throughout school and who were hoping to improve their grade record with an additional year of study. For six weeks I used the traditional approach to teaching speech: demonstration, textbook readings, speech assignments, and presentations. By the end of the six weeks, the students were as "turned off" as when they had entered the class.

In search of a new approach, I chose a number of projects involving media. Each student was assigned to write and tape a commercial on a product of his own choosing. Students were also asked to prepare a slide-tape presentation on a subject of particular interest. One football player enrolled in the class did his presentation on art history; another student, admired as one of the top wrestlers in the school, depicted the spiritual life of the youth of America.

Another project was a group effort culminating in a ten-minute televised instructional program. To accomplish this goal, the students learned storyboarding, scripting, operation of the videotape recorder and camera equipment, and how to involve others at the academy to help in their presentation. Their final projects took the form of 8mm films on such topics as wrestling and weightlifting.

The new approach had worked as I had hoped. The students became totally consumed by their assignments and even managed to spread their enthusiasm to other students and to the faculty as well. While nonprint media was used as a focal point, the students had to rely heavily on print in order to complete their projects. The use of media served as a source of motivation for a wider use of print.

I encountered a similar experience when I served as media librarian for a small rural elementary school. A fourth grade teacher approached me one day for help with a number of students she termed "reluctant readers." Their history of failures and a moderate amount of name calling by other students in the school had convinced them that they were at the "bottom of the heap."

Although I had never attempted to produce a filmstrip with such a young group, we decided to devote 30 minutes each day for a period of two weeks to such a project. The final product was to be shown to the Parent Teachers Organization. Students were organized into committees with responsibilities for art, script, layout, and filming. In addition, each child was responsible for the design and script for one frame. Students who had shown great reluctance to use books, encyclopedias, or even magazines, now devoured the printed page for information to be used in their filmstrip frame. The final product was both an individual and a group success. The recognition gained from other students and from the parents further reinforced the satisfactions that the students had gained from their research.

While much has been said and written about the advantages of using media with gifted or bright students, I believe it offers many benefits for the "turned off" or slower student as well. The use of media should be considered an avenue through which print can become more attractive and more meaningful to the student.

If I Read This Book . . . Do I Have to Write a Book Report?

by Carolyn Paine

The slightest suspicion that the reading of a book might lead directly to a sit-down-and-write assignment can make "reading for pleasure" something less than billed. So it might comfort your cautious recreational readers a bit to hear that while there'll be some sort of follow-up sharing on books (I knew it!), it won't be the kind of book reporting you think (Oh?). Alternatives to standard book reporting—a task that seems to have a decidedly dampening effect on carefully kindled reading enthusiasm—might provide a needed spark for many recreational reading programs.

READING UNDERCOVER

Melody Dian of Crown Point, Indiana, suggests a "Secret Library Pal" Project. The class draws names. Then each student sets out, in undercover fashion, to discover the interests of his or her library pal, to determine the sort of book that person might enjoy.

Each student picks out, checks out, and reads a library book for his or her pal. The next step is for the student to make up a list of six or seven questions relating to the book. (You may want to guide this question-writing phase, helping students include "why" or "what do you think" questions as well as questions dealing with straight facts about the books.) Each set of questions is then put into an envelope and slid into its respective book. Then the book-and-envelope sets are presented to the library pals.

After the pals have had a chance to read the books chosen for them, pairs of students who've now read the same books get together to discuss the answers to the questions. There'll be two discussion sessions for each student, because each drew someone and was drawn by someone.

Besides heightening interest in reading, this kind of book sharing can help broaden some reading habits—moving some students out of horse stories, for the moment, and into mysteries, or out of science fiction and into Black history—expanding and enriching everyone's reading menu.

HOW TO POCKET A FEW SKILLS

Robert Hillerich, Professor of Education at Bowling Green State University in Bowling Green, Ohio, suggests that teachers "card" a few library books with mini-activity slips. All it takes is a stack of 3 x 5 cards and some carefully prepared questions or activities relating to a few selected books. (Of course, there may be an occasional bright-eyes in your class who'll make it a point to start inspecting card pockets before selecting a library book, choosing not to choose those that call for extra work.)

The questions/activities you'll be preparing could be specially constructed to give practice in particular reading comprehension skills, rather than simply to inquire into the who-what-when of the story. For instance, one question on the card might involve drawing conclusions from the reading; another, predicting an outcome; a third, identifying the main idea or interpreting figurative language. You also might suggest an activity growing out of the reading, such as drawing the most exciting (funniest, saddest) moment in the story, or briefly telling a new adventure the main character might have.

To provide a self-check (for questions that have specific answers) you might: (1) prepare a separate card that could also be placed in the book pocket, (2) put answers on the back of the activity card, or (3) make a notebook with answers listed under alphabetically arranged titles.

When students become accustomed to using these cards, they may try supplying similar activity cards for some uncarded books they may read. Discuss some of the kinds of questions they might try. Vocabulary-in-context questions make simple and useful starters.

TELL IT WITH PICTURES

James Abbott, Coordinator of Early Childhood Education at the 32nd Street School in Los Angeles, finds pictorial book reporting useful. The reader/reporter is asked first to think through the story in order to recall important events and memorable scenes. The student then selects six favorite scenes to illustrate, leaving space on each picture to write a caption—a sentence explaining or expanding upon what is happening in the picture. The finished scenes can then be assembled in sequential order and fastened together to make a book, or taped side-by-side to make a six-panel display. A cover sheet (or first panel) carrying the title and author of the book can be added to complete the pictorial report.

PEN PAL REVIEWS

Margaret Langford, who teaches reading to sixth graders at Fort Stockton Junior High in Fort Stockton, Texas, gives book reporting a correspondence angle. Each reader, after completing a basic book information sheet (title, author, kind of book, etc.), puts some of his or her thoughts about the book into a letter addressed to a student in another classroom. The letters aren't supposed to sound like literary reviews, of course. Students write real letters about all kinds of things, with book comments included as only one part of the message.

This is a fine chance for a quick brush-up on letter-writing and envelope-writing forms and formats too. Special stationery can make the occasion more fun, and the doodlers and decorators in the group can be invited to draw and color away as they like. Delivery of this mail can be a specially awarded responsibility.

Pen-pal book reports give students a chance to show off what they know, and the activity may lead to more letter exchanging as well as fulfilling its book-boosting mission.

A QUILT THAT SPREADS THE WORD

Dorean Kimball, a teacher at Central Elementary School in Penacook, New Hampshire, has a plan that helps students keep track of their library reading, and at the same time encourages further reading by helping to spread the word about books students have enjoyed. Each book finisher gets a chance to create a quilt square to represent the just-read book, then adds the square to a growing patchwork reading quilt.

Provide white construction paper cut into 9 x 9-inch squares. The block should be designed by the student in such a way that it can carry the book's title and author. (Students can include their own names or not, as they choose.) But the major portion of the square will be devoted to an illustration or design that suggests what impressed the reader most about that book. The artwork can be done in crayon, tempera, or may be assembled from cut paper—for that authentic, pieced-together look.

Each student also prepares a paragraph or two telling about the book and perhaps explaining the symbolism used in his or her quilt block. These paragraphs, keyed to the appropriate quilt blocks by number, are collected into a reference notebook that should be stationed near the quilt display. These reports are for the benefit of others who, intrigued by some quilt block, may want to see what the book behind it has in store.

The ever-expanding quilt may occupy a fair amount of wall space, something that needs to be planned for. But as a reference work, an appealing piece of art, or even an open-house conversation piece, the patchwork reading quilt earns its territory.

WHAT'S YOUR BAG?

Students of L. Whitman of Mayfield, New York, put together brown-bag book reports. Children who want to tell about books they've read get to illustrate their book talks with objects they've collected for that purpose and stored in a big brown bag. These book-talk visual aids range from stuffed animals or other toys to household items, drawings, constructions, mounted cutouts from magazines, flowers, stones—whatever helps illustrate the characters, setting, or action of the book.

As children talk about their books, they reveal the in-the-bag items, one by one, at appropriate spots. Children should have worked ahead of time with their chosen items to help smooth out the sequencing and polish the presentation. (The surprises should be for the audience, not the speaker.) Some collections may lend themselves later on to displays or collages to represent the book—with a label revealing the title and author as a reference for others.

Not every book needs reporting on. Most *free* reading should be just that. But when book sharing times do come along—opportunities rendered more special by their just-once-in-a-while status—the chance for choice in format for presenting information, thoughts, opinions, and feelings about books could be most welcome—for reporter and report-receiver alike.

Child's Play: Games to Teach Reading

by Karen Steiner

Games and simulations are excellent tools for stimulating student motivation, ensuring active student participation, and reinforcing specific skills and concepts in many subjects. In recent years, many reading teachers recognizing these benefits have adopted the use of games to enhance reading skill development, a process which is too often relegated to the instructional backseat of drill and repetition. It is hoped that the following resources gleaned from the Educational Resources Information Center (ERIC) data base will encourage more teachers to incorporate games and simulations into their classrooms and to create new systems of their own.

The rationale which underlies the use of educational games in the classroom can perhaps also account for the increased interest in their use. As Dwayne C. Poll notes in "Gaming in the Language Arts," "In the American school, the teacher is the focal point of the teaching/learning process."[1] Recent experimentation with educational alternatives such as independent study and the open classroom reflects a dissatisfaction with this role conception. Gaming activities, if nothing else, reorient the teacher's responsibility: he or she becomes a facilitator of learning, not the sole dispenser of it. In many ways, the use of games and simulations in the classroom indicates the belief that students can and must be responsible for their own learning—that, in fact, they learn best by taking an active part in their own education.

Poll's exercise "Walking Words," illustrates this type of thinking. In this game, children are introduced to the concept of synonym groups through creative dramatics. As they walk in a circle, they are asked if they can *sneak* as if they did not want anyone to see them, *march* like soldiers, *tramp* like noisy boys, and *scamper* like puppies. This exercise can easily be adapted to illustrate the meaning of other groups of words.

GAMES FOR READING READINESS

Games may also be used to develop reading readiness skills in pre-school children. In "Games Graffiti: Language Arts Games to Make for Young Children," Mary Anne Christenberry and others suggest ways for parents and teachers to encourage the formation of organizational patterns essential to beginning reading.[2] These exercises are based on the Piagetian concept that it is "imperative for children to interact with real objects in order to learn about and, indeed, to create their cognitive world." Mastery of three basic concepts is urged: (1) grouping by shape, color, and size; (2) grouping according to identity; and (3) grouping according to other, more complex, relationships. Exercises, intended primarily for individual use but adaptable to the small group setting, utilize familiar objects and materials to achieve this goal. Shadow-matching, a game designed to encourage comparison by shape, is made from tagboard. An exercise illustrating the idea that "separate parts can be arranged to form a meaningful whole" is created from magazine pictures which are cut to make a simple puzzle.

Often, the creation of effective teaching games comes naturally from children's and teachers' interaction in the classroom itself. *Elephant Walk, the Wig Shop, and Other Reading Games Children Play* by Edwardene Armstrong is a collection of 49 strategies created by reading aides in the ESEA Title I Primary Reading Program in Omaha, Nebraska.[3] Intended to provide practice and mastery of specific reading skills, games are grouped according to the following reading skill categories: alphabet, consonants, digraphs, rhyming words, and vowels. An illustration is provided for each game, and lists of necessary materials are included with instructions for making the games. An example of one such exercise is a modification of the familiar game of concentration: In order to encourage the development of sight word vocabulary, at least 20 words from a currently used reading text are selected. A pair of cards is made for each word. Each of from two to four players chooses a numbered card displayed on the game board, pronounces the word written on the back, and attempts to match the word with another card from the game board. At the end of the game, the player with the most cards is the winner.

ADAPTING POPULAR GAMES

Many popular games can be adapted in this manner to reinforce reading skills. *Skill Cards for Open-Ended Gameboards, Set A* provides question and answer cards which can be used to establish the criteria for taking a turn in any kind of open-ended game.[4] Twelve sets of cards span such topics as long vowel substitution, short vowel substitution, consonant digraph substitution, consonant substitution, and consonant blend substitution. Each set contains 20 skill cards and one answer card. By using games that are already part of children's repertoires or games that have an innate appeal, the teacher can readily tap an established source of student motivation.

In *Commercial Games—Made Relevant for Reading,* George Canney suggests that almost any game can be turned into a reading or content area game if students are required, before taking a turn, to read a word, identify a suffix, spell a word, or punctuate a sentence.[5] The author notes that students are frequently more challenged by the game situation than they are by the seatwork exercises typically employed to practice skills. Guidelines for the adaptation of commercial games to the reading classsroom include the suggestion that teachers construct few, if any, game boards. (The attractiveness and visual appeal of commercially produced games may be a motivator for children.) In addition, Canney proposes that games which incorporate an element of surprise (and even occasional destruction) are valuable. The time element must also be considered; too much time spent in waiting for a turn can minimize instructional benefits. A list of games which fulfill these requirements, organized according to their appropriateness for primary and secondary students, includes Chutes and Ladders, Scrabble Alphabet, Guinness Book of World Records, and Bingo. Price and availability information for each game is provided.

An additional caution expressed by Canney concerning the use of reading games is also shared by Michael E. Currier, author of "Five Fingers: Games and Activities to Motivate the Growing Reader."[6] Games, they assert, should not be used to *teach* specific reading skills. Rather, games achieve their greatest effectiveness when used to *reinforce* skills that have already been presented in another instructional framework. The diagnostic value of learning games is also, according to Currier, seriously underestimated. The gaming situation can offer the opportunity for teachers to assess both cognitive and affective functioning under less artificial circumstances than are present in traditional testing. Social behavior, problem solving tactics, competitive behavior, and other interactional patterns are some of the characteristics that can be readily evaluated.

OUTLET FOR ENERGY

One exercise from this extensive collection, Bean Bag Phonics, illustrates yet another benefit that can be gained from the use of classroom games: movement. At a distance of 6 to 10 feet, players toss bean bags at containers labeled with varying criteria for words (the inclusion of specific vowels, use of hard and soft consonants, and so on). When a bean bag lands in a container, the player must say a word satisfying the established criteria. Games that involve children actively in this manner can effectively direct energy into constructive channels. Yet another exercise from this collection makes use of children's natural fascination for riddles. In Riddle Me

Please, riddles and their answers are written on color coded strips of construction paper. Strips are shuffled and passed around the group. In turn, each child reads a riddle aloud and others are given an opportunity to answer. At the end of play, a winner may be determined by who gets rid of all of his or her strips first, or by who collects the greatest number of complete riddles.

Games may easily be adapted to the reading class that employs a learning center approach, as "Ideas for Reading Learning Centers" illustrates.[7] Activities are divided into the categories of reading readiness, vocabulary, phonetic analysis, structural analysis, comprehension, creative writing, and study skills. Among the approximately 100 ideas presented in this work is Silent Auction, a game to encourage children to write complete sentences. In this game, students attempt to identify the contents of a sealed box by shaking it. Several small items—a sock, a jacks ball, a clothespin, and so on—can be placed inside the box, one at a time. Students then compose a sentence speculating on the nature of the item. Criteria for the sentences can be varied according to the sophistication of the group in question, and the mystery box can form the basis for a weekly class activity.

The possibilities for creating and modifying games to reinforce reading skills are seemingly endless and can include the use of children's own favorite activities as well as teacher-developed or commercially produced materials. For example, children's oral expression in play, such as jump rope rhymes or the words that traditionally accompany hide-and-seek, can provide a rich source of ideas for relating games and gaming to language use. And despite criticisms leveled against their use—that they teach competition, simplify the world unnecessarily, and avoid issues in "real learning"—games possess an undeniable ability to motivate and to involve that cannot be ignored.

NOTES

1. Dwayne C. Poll, "Gaming in the Language Arts," *Elementary English* 50 (1973): 535-38, 48.
2. Mary Anne Christenberry, et al., "Games Graffiti: Language Arts Games to Make for Young Children." Paper presented at the Annual Meeting of the International Reading Association, Anaheim, CA, 1976.
3. Edwardene Armstrong, *Elephant Walk, the Wig Shop, and Other Reading Games Children Play* (Omaha, NE: Omaha Public Schools, 1975).
4. *Skill Cards for Open-Ended Gameboards, Set A* (Newport Beach, CA: California Reading Association, 1975).
5. George Canney, *Commercial Games—Made Relevant for Reading* (Urbana, IL, 1976) ERIC ED 131 424.

6. Michael E. Currier, ''Five Fingers: Games and Activities to Motivate the Growing Reader.'' Paper presented at the Fourth Plains Regional Conference of the International Reading Association, Wichita, KS: 1976. Also available from Armbrust Educational Publishers.

7. *Ideas for Reading Learning Centers* (Newport Beach, CA: California Reading Association, 1973).

Commercial Games—Made Relevant for Reading

by George Canney

It is the purpose of this article to suggest a means to effectively integrate reading games into the curriculum and to do so both from a theoretical position and from a highly pragmatic view. Sensibly constructed, such games can be infused into the daily lesson plan as supplemental practice assignments, or incorporated into learning centers to reinforce skills previously introduced.

In order to learn to read, most children must spend a rather lengthy time practicing various word recognition skills. However, if they approach these practice exercises without much interest and are easily distracted, learning is minimized. To be effective, the practice must attract children's attention, challenge them to use their knowledge to respond, and lead them to determine the answers most appropriate for the exercise.

Unfortunately, for many children the typical seatwork exercises employed to practice skills introduced by the teacher neither attract children's attention nor challenge them to respond. These children often answer the question passively, uncritically, and with little concern for the reasonableness of their answers.

In contrast, reading games often provoke interest, even excitement, among the players and provide strong motivation to give correct answers. Skills introduced earlier through direct instruction are consciously and purposely rehearsed by students who frequently respond in an unthinking fashion to similar questions on a dittoed worksheet. Games, therefore, can be an effective means to help students learn basic skills to automaticity, a performance level seen by LaBerge and Samuels to be necessary for fluent reading to occur.[1]

Of course, to be effective, the reading games, like all practice activities, ought to be constructed to maximize the transfer of skills to the child's own reading. As Smith suggested,[2] such games should minimize the presentation of words in isolation (see Figure 1), should maximize the amount of time each child can respond, and should avoid being so contrived that nontransferable associations are built between the words and the context in which they are learned (the games).

The approach being proposed is a simple one: almost any game of interest to children can be turned into a reading or content area game if, before taking a turn, the pupil is required to read a word, identify a suffix, match homonym pairs, spell a word, punctuate a sentence, answer a question and so on.

In order to enhance the instructional value of such *reading games*, these six rules need to be considered:

1. Teachers should construct few, if any, game boards. Commercially prepared games (not reading games per se) are usually more attractive, more durable, and often no more expensive to acquire than teacher-made games. When the time to make a game board is considered along with the cost of the materials, it is seldom the case that the teacher-made game costs less to make than the commercial game. Exceptions to this rule apply in instances when the teacher chooses to make a game board either because the game is unavailable commercially or because the teacher is attempting to convince a reluctant reader s/he is important.

2. Choose games which incorporate the element of *surprise*, or chance, so that when one player falls behind, s/he still has an opportunity to win. Examples: *Chutes and Ladders, Sorry, Clue*. When a game does not hold surprise, as one player pulls ahead the other players lose interest in the game and are less motivated to give sensible answers to the reading questions. Under such circumstances, learning is minimized.

3. Occasionally use games which include some opportunities for *destruction*, especially when the time to take a turn is brief (see rule 5). Games which permit the players to knock over some targets, throw an object, or disrupt some organization are appealing to most age groups. Examples: *Don't Break the Ice, Don't Cook Your Goose, London Bridge*.

4. Regardless of the game selected, it is seldom advisable to have more than three players participating. When there are more than three players, too much instructional time is wasted in waiting for a turn. Exceptions: *Bingo, One-Minute Scrabble*.

5. For any game you select, the time needed to take a turn ought to be minimal relative to the time needed to complete the required reading task for the reasons just stated in rule 4. Examples: *Checkers*, many board games, but not *Monopoly, Tiddly Winks*, or pitching horseshoes.

6. The gaming situation should not be used to introduce new skills. Rather, the skills being practiced in the gaming situation are those that have been previously introduced and practiced such that the pupil can select most of the correct responses when they are present.

Ten to fifteen popular games with the characteristics mentioned above are sufficient to initiate a reading skills center. In addition to these games, any number of word card games, such as fish, rummy, concentration, and *Word-O,* may be added to the skills center. The procedure for turning a commercial game into a reading game is simple. Under no circumstances should specific letters, spelling patterns, or vocabulary items be written on the gaming materials. Instead, the teacher should put all the skills to be practiced on 2½ x 3 inch cards which can be purchased in a variety of colors from printing companies at a cost of around $5.25 per 1000 cards.

Decks of cards are constructed to include from 20 to 50 cards (fewer cards for younger or less able readers). The cards are coded on one side for identification purposes and are numbered on the other side when an answer key is included. On the numbered side of the card the reading item is neatly printed or typed. (See Figure 1.) Card decks can be developed which deal with the visual recognition of grapheme patterns, various structural analysis skills, punctuation, definitions, classification skills, vocabulary, and spelling.

The code used to identify the skills covered and difficulty levels of the individual card decks is a simple one. For example, the card in Figure 1 is coded VH2 to stand for vocabulary (V), homonyms (H), at difficulty level two (2). It is the teacher who determines the difficulty levels appropriate for the materials s/he is using and his/her pupils. A ringbinder can be used as a catalog to store a record sheet for each skill category (vocabulary, initial consonant clusters, long vowel patterns, spelling, punctuation, classification, etc.). Each sheet is organized in outline fashion by skill-subskill-difficulty category and is continually updated as new card decks and activities other than games are added.

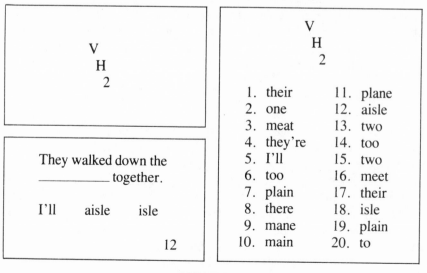

FIGURE 1

If a pupil is expected to simply read a word, then it is necessary that at least one other player be at a comparable reading level in order to determine if the pupil correctly decoded the word. If a pupil is to spell a word, then the opponent draws the card and reads it to the player; the card itself is the answer key. For the remaining reading skills, an answer key like the one shown in Figure 1 may be used by the opponent to determine the correctness of the player's answer.

The instances in which these checking systems fail are few, since the card decks contain items which have already been introduced and practiced with the teacher present. Every incorrect answer is immediately corrected and the card returned to the deck to be drawn again. In this way, each player is encouraged to rehearse the correct response because s/he will soon draw the same card again.

The reasons for utilizing this approach to reinforce basic reading skills are numerous, especially when the games are incorporated into a learning center.

First, in order to develop card decks to use with commercial games, the teacher must be knowledgeable about the scope and the sequence of the materials s/he is using. One outcome of this careful study is increased attention to the strengths and weaknesses of the reading program, including concern for the quality and quantity of practice exercises designed to strengthen pupils' command of basic reading skills.

Second, by constructing card decks which focus on a narrow range of skills found in the reading materials, the teacher can provide appropriate amounts of practice at the right time for individual pupils. Unlike commercially prepared reading games, which usually present too broad a sample of items for a specific skill (e.g., *all* the initial consonant clusters, all homonyms) and may not follow the scope and sequence of the reading materials being used in a classroom, teacher-made card decks to accompany unaltered commercial games can be constructed to offer high density relevant practice when it is most productive.

Third, through the use of special card decks, children differing widely in reading level can practice together on an equal basis. They learn to assist one another in improving their reading performance and to realize that the teacher is not the only person having the correct answers.

Fourth, most children make every effort to give the correct response called for in the card and to avoid repeating earlier mistakes in order to win the game they are playing. Since it is the teacher who assigns the card decks to be used, his/her observation of how well the pupil performs on his/her own provides feedback about how effectively the pupil can utilize previous instruction and practice. In a sense, the child's performance in this type of activity is one measure of transfer of instruction into the pupil's own reading strategies.

Fifth, pupils are strongly motivated to do the assigned reading task and persist until the exercise is completed. Since the reading skills and vocabulary have already been introduced and practiced, the gaming situation seems less like a test of what the child doesn't know and more like a confirmation of what s/he has learned.

Sixth, the pupil is allowed to choose the game s/he wants and, in most instances, with whom s/he wishes to play. The emphasis is on the child assuming some responsibility for what s/he is learning and therefore for completing the chosen activity in an acceptable fashion within the time allotted. Such learning experiences tend to foster independence and some recognition of the fact that it is primarily the child, and not the teacher, who is the learner. Also, since the children select the games they wish to play, while the teacher assigns the specific card deck to use, most children are eager to stay on task and complete the assignments *because they choose to do it!*

A teacher-structured gaming program can be effectively monitored by older students, parent volunteers and, yes, even school social workers, principals, and other interested adults to provide more assistance for individual pupils when they need it. This is possible because the reading skills have been previously introduced to and practiced by the pupil, because most of the card decks have answer keys held by the opponent, because most adults are in a position to recognize a correct response when they hear it, and because the teacher is responsible for assigning each pupil to a skill and level appropriate for that child.

In order to effectively and efficiently implement this approach to skills instruction within a learning center, the teacher should consider these four steps.

First, some type of record-keeping system is advisable so that the teacher can assign to each pupil particular card decks dealing with specific reading skills, which may or may not be appropriate for other pupils reading at the same level. Unless some form of record keeping is used, it is unlikely that a teacher could assign each child in the class to an appropriate skill at the time when practice would be most effective—and do so week after week.

Second, a prescription card should be developed to serve both as a written assignment sheet for the pupil and as a record of which skills, or centers, each pupil was assigned and some evaluation of how the student performed.

If, over time, centers are constructed within or across classrooms so that different skills are being practiced (e.g., spelling, prefixes and suffixes, predictable patterns, sight vocabulary, creative writing, comprehension, study skills, etc.), then a prescription card/record sheet like that in Figure 2 becomes highly functional.

Name **Bobby J.**

Date **April** Room **212**

Skill Centers / Week	Consonant Clusters	Predictable Patterns	Sight Words	Vowel Clusters	Spelling	Punctuation	Prefixes & Suffixes	Comprehension
6				worked well	II_A		fine	IV
Initials					C.C.			L.K.
9				I_{C_2}	ok – send ask		II_A too hard	
Initials				R.J.			L.K.	
13	II_B	ok					II_A 2 didn't finish	
Initials	J.C.					Z.L.		
16				I_{C_2} fine			I_C ok – enjoyed task	
Initials			R.J.				L.K.	

KEY

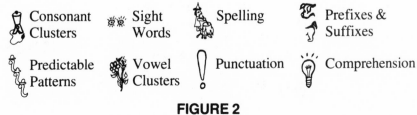

Consonant Clusters Sight Words Spelling Prefixes & Suffixes

Predictable Patterns Vowel Clusters Punctuation Comprehension

FIGURE 2

The prescription sheet can be filled in by the teacher on a biweekly basis. The initials below each assigned center confirm the fact that the pupil did complete the activity. By examining the comments written next to the skill center picture by the teacher, by the adult or student volunteer, or by the pupil himself/herself, the teacher can reassign the pupil to the same level, to different levels within a particular skill center, or to other centers. The comments are diagnostic in character, but simple: too easy; too hard; send back again; worked well; fine, etc.

Third, the implementation of a gaming approach requires planning, time to develop card decks and materials commonly found in learning centers, and careful record keeping. It makes sense, then, to utilize these materials in lieu of some of the more traditional seatwork activities, and to do so frequently enough to warrant the effort expended. These materials are not meant to be used after a child's work is done, or as an occasional Friday afternoon treat. Rather, by following the procedures suggested here, games can be an effective part of the regular reading program, to be used once or twice a week for as long as an hour with children at all reading levels. When sensibly sequenced, carefully constructed, and regularly evaluated, the gaming approach will incite pupils to willingly and thoughtfully practice basic reading skills normally considered by many children, especially average and low readers, to be dull and senseless.

Finally, the materials needed to initiate a gaming approach can be acquired inexpensively through a variety of sources for under $50.00. Typically, a collection of games like those listed in Figure 3 is sufficient to initiate a center.

What has been suggested is that all too often children are required to practice basic reading skills using prescribed materials which do little to motivate them to attend, to think, to learn. The pupils rarely are given a choice of activities and often receive additional work of a similar character when they complete their assignments. Games, on the other hand, are exciting, fun to play, and hold children's attention. By associating basic skills with games—games which the children choose to play—most pupils become highly motivated to continually practice basic skills until those skills become automatic. In fact, the more automatic those skills become, the better the pupils like it because they seldom miss a turn, and, more significantly, they can see the development of their own reading proficiency. While no one approach has ever been demonstrated to be effective for all pupils all the time, it is hoped that you will give serious consideration to the incorporation of commercially developed games into your reading program. Used sensibly they do make a difference!

PRIMARY

Title	Publisher	Approximate Cost
Chutes and Ladders	Milton-Bradley (MB)	$2.98
Walk Along Sesame Street	MB	3.88
Raggedy Ann	MB	2.99
Candyland	MB	3.29
Yogi Bear	MB	1.25
Casper the Friendly Ghost	MB	1.25
Land of the Lost	MB	1.90
Pizza Pie Game	MB	5.03
The Great Grape Ape	MB	1.25
Checkers (2 sets)	MB	2.00
Cootie	Schaper (S)	3.25
London Bridge	S	4.99
Humpty-Dumpty	S	3.98
Don't Break the Ice	S	4.66
Hi-Ho Cherry-O	Whitman	1.88
Scrabble Alphabet Game	Selchow & Righter	4.77
Bingo	(teacher made)	- - -
Concentration game boards	(teacher made)	.50
Assorted word card games	(teacher made)	- - -
		$49.55

INTERMEDIATE

Chutes and Ladders	Milton-Bradley (MB)	2.98
Go to the Head of the Class	MB	4.99
Speed Buggy	MB	1.25
Scooby Doo	MB	1.23
Emergency	MB	2.99
Homestretch	MB	2.90
Planet of the Apes	MB	2.90
Korg—70,000 B.C.	MB	1.90
Checkers	MB	1.00
Guinness Book of Records Game	Parker Brothers (PB)	6.79
Scrabble Got a Minute	Selchow & Righter	2.98
Kerplunk	Ideal	5.96
Tip-It	Ideal	2.90
Don't Break the Ice	Schaper (S)	4.66
Don't Cook Your Goose	S	3.98
Bingo	(teacher made)	- - -
Concentration game boards	(teacher made)	.50
Assorted word card games	(teacher made)	- - -
		$49.91

FIGURE 3

REFERENCES

1. D. LaBerge and J. Samuels, "Toward a Theory of Automatic Information Processing in Reading," *Cognitive Psychology* 6 (1974): 293-323.
2. Nila Banton Smith, *Reading Instruction for Today's Children* (Englewood Cliffs,NJ: Prentice-Hall, 1963), pp. 173-75.

MATERIALS

Checkers. Racine, WI: Western Publishing, 1975.
Chutes and Ladders. Springfield, MA: Milton Bradley, 1976.
Clue. Salem, MA: Parker Brothers, 1976.
Don't Break the Ice. Minneapolis, MN: Schaper, 1976.
Don't Cook Your Goose. Minneapolis, MN: Schaper, 1976.
London Bridge. Minneapolis, MN: Schaper, 1976.
Monopoly. Salem, MA: Parker Brothers, 1975.
Scrabble Got a Minute. Bay Shore, NY: Selchow & Righter, 1973.

APPENDICES

Glossary

The following terms have been defined according to their usage in this text and are provided for the reader's clarification:

Elementary Age Pupil: Elementary school generally comprises the first five or six years of public school in the United States. A student or pupil of elementary age would be approximately six through twelve years of age.

Grades: Public education in the United States generally encompasses 12 grades. Children enter 1st grade at the age of six and graduate after completing the 12th grade at the age of seventeen or eighteen. Each grade level takes approximately one academic year or nine months to complete. In general: grades 1 through 3 are often referred to as the *primary grades;* grades 4 through 6 are *upper elementary; junior high* comprises grades 7 through 9; and *high school* refers to grades 10 through 12. In some school systems a *middle school* is also included which takes in grades 6 through 8. The *junior high* is then eliminated and *high school* becomes grades 9 through 12.

High School: The last three to four years of public school in the United States, made up of grades 9 through 12, are referred to as *high school.* Successful completion of grade 12 results in the awarding of a diploma and the student is said to have been *graduated.*

Middle Level Classrooms: Classrooms in which students are in grades 6 through 8 are often referred to as middle level classrooms. Pupils at this level would be approximately 11 through 13 years of age.

Middle School: While there may be some geographical variations, middle school in the United States usually consists of grades 6 through 8. The term *middle school* was used because of its placement between elementary and high school.

Newbery: The Newbery Medal is an award given by the Association for Library Service to Children of the American Library Association to "the author of the most distinguished contribution to American literature for children." It has been awarded annually since 1922. Books receiving this medal are often referred to as "Newberys."

Student: An individual of any age engaged in some type of formal education might be called a *student*. The terms *student* and *pupil* are used interchangeably when referring to individuals progressing through the 12 years of public school.

Young Adult: An individual of middle school age or older might be referred to as a *young adult*. Young adulthood is roughly analogous to the period of adolescence.

Bibliography

While only journal articles have been selected for inclusion in this text, the following annotated bibliography includes books that cover specific techniques used to motivate students to read. Also listed are a few recent activity-oriented titles which the editors have used in their approaches to stimulating reading interests in children and young adults. A few of the books included are out-of-print as indicated in the bibliographic data; however, these were considered as valuable tools for building a collection in the area. Additionally, six articles have been listed which did not fall into any of the major categories covered in this work.

Adler, Mortimer J. and Van Doren, Charles. *How to Read a Book*. New York: Simon and Schuster, 1972.
The authors discuss principles of effective reading in terms of four basic levels: elementary, inspectional, analytical, and syntopical. Emphasis is placed on being an active, demanding, and critical reader.

Alexander, J. Estill and Filler, Ronald Claude. *Attitudes and Reading*. Newark, DE: International Reading Association, 1976.
The authors set forth ways to develop and maintain positive self-concepts and attitudes in youngsters toward reading. A teacher and attitudes checklist as assessment instruments is also given.

Caney, Steven. *Kids' America*. New York: Workman Publishing, 1978.
Kids' America is a survey of American life through things to make and do by and with children. The book is divided into 11 chapters which cover such topics as genealogy, backyard fun, fashion, diet, arts and crafts, and playthings. Any one of these chapters might serve as a beginning activity to introduce a variety of reading units dealing with American history, ingenuity, and life-styles.

————. *Steven Caney's Playbook*. New York: Workman Publishing, 1975.
Seventy activities, games, projects, tricks, puzzles, toys, and recipes are discussed for children three years of age and older. The text is accompanied by pictures and detailed illustrations.

Carlsen, G. Robert. *Books and the Teen-Age Reader*. 2d ed., rev. New York: Harper & Row, 1972.
The author surveys a variety of motivational factors which might influence the young adult's reading experience. He also analyzes "the teen-ager and his world"

and sets forth three stages of reading development beginning with early adolescence (age 11) through late adolescence (age 18). Different types of literature are discussed as they relate to the young adult. An annotated bibliography is attached after each type.

Chambers, Dewey W. *Children's Literature in the Curriculum*. Chicago: Rand McNally, 1971. (Out of Print)

The importance of children's literature to the elementary curriculum is emphasized. The author also discusses how children's literature can spark creative, divergent thinking for the age group.

Cleary, Florence Damon. *Blueprints for Better Reading; School Programs for Promoting Skill and Interest in Reading*. 2d ed. New York: H.W. Wilson, 1972.

The book is divided into three main sections: reading guidance, approaches to reading guidance programs, and programs in reading guidance. The last section is particularly valuable since the author discusses a variety of programs using literature to motivate young people to read.

————. *Discovering Books and Libraries; A Handbook for Students in the Middle and Upper Grades*. 2d ed. New York: H.W. Wilson, 1977.

The title indicates the purpose of this book: "A handbook for *students*" to use in all areas of book selection and evaluation. In addition to its usefulness as a reference tool for learning how to use the library, the specific chapter on "You and Your Reading" suggests ways that students should go about choosing the right book.

Donelson, Kenneth L., ed. and the Committee on the Senior High School Booklist. *Books for You: A Booklist for Senior High Students*. Urbana, IL: NCTE, 1976.

This book list with descriptive annotations for each title is intended for use by senior high students "with all sorts of interests." The list is divided into 43 subjects that cover a variety of areas important to the young adult, such as "Love," "I Am Woman," "Careers," "Sports" and "Problems and Young People."

Edwards, Margaret A. *The Fair Garden and the Swarm of Beasts*. New York: Hawthorne Books, 1974. (Out of Print)

Insights and recommendations from an experienced librarian are given for working with a wide variety of programs for young adults. Especially useful is the "practical appendix" titled "The Tool Shed," which contains ideas on book selection, book talks, book discussions, use of paperbacks, films and other media, and reading lists to be used in motivating what she calls the teenage "beasts" to read.

Estes, Thomas H. "A Scale to Measure Attitudes toward Reading." *Journal of Reading* 15 (November 1971): 135-38.

A proposed scale for measuring attitudes toward reading is offered along with an explanation of its development. Administration of a pre- and post-test is recommended to note changes in attitudes. An updated version of this scale—*Estes*

Attitude Scale—is available from Charlottesville, VA: Virginia Research Associates, 1975.

Fader, Daniel N. *The New Hooked on Books*. New York: Berkley Publishing, 1976.
This is a revised edition of the 1968 version with an updated reading list. The author discusses a variety of student-tested approaches to hook young people on reading. Examples of successful programs are given as models.

Forte, Imogene; Frank, Marjorie; and MacKenzie, Joy. *Kids' Stuff: Reading and Language Experiences*. Nashville: Incentive Publications, 1974.
The numerous activities in this work designed for intermediate grades include for each a specific purpose and step-by-step procedures. Variations in level of difficulty are suggested. Areas covered include reading, speaking and listening, spelling and writing.

Greenlaw, M. Jean and Carswell, Margaret D. "Think Thin: Some Good Short Books." *School Library Journal* 25 (December 1978): 32-33.
The annotated book list of "thin" books is appropriate for grades 2-7. The list is intended "as a springboard" to other books and is designed for youngsters reluctant to read books which "appear" to be too long and too complicated to enjoy.

Harris, Albert J. and Sipay, Edward R. *How to Increase Your Reading Ability*. 6th ed. New York: David McKay, 1975.
While this book might serve as a reference tool in reading, Chapter 13 includes a section titled "Principles of effective motivation" which deals with methods of motivating the reluctant reader.

Johns, Jerry L. "Motivating Reluctant Readers." *Journal of Research and Development in Education* 11 (1978): 69-74.
Who are reluctant readers? Why are some students reluctant readers? What can be done to motivate them? Johns addresses these questions and offers suggestions based on the most recent research.

Pilgrim, Geneva Hanna and McAllister, Mariana K. *Books, Young People, and Reading Guidance*. 2d ed. New York: Harper & Row, 1968. (Out of Print)
This work is written for the adult who will be working with young people in guiding their choices of reading materials. It surveys the literature available for young adults, reading interests and needs of this group, and book selection. A recommended list of books mentioned in the text is also included.

Polette, Nancy and Hamlin, Marjorie. *Reading Guidance in a Media Age*. Metuchen, NJ: Scarecrow Press, 1975.
The authors share their insights into ways young people may be guided to become involved with the reading experience. A variety of topics are included, such as the influence of the home, ways the library can capture readers, independent reading programs, and student audiovisual productions with literature. Each chapter is followed by a bibliographic listing of books mentioned within the chapter.

Reid, Virginia, ed. *Reading Ladders for Human Relations*. 5th ed. Washington, DC: American Council on Education, 1972.

This is a work intended "to advance the cause of better human relations" by listing books "that may increase the social sensitivity of young people and to extend their experience, appreciation, and understanding of their own life styles and the life styles of others." In addition to the four themes developed around an extensive annotated book list of recommended titles for use with primary through senior high level students, the editor has included in the introduction to the book "ways of working with young people and books," "book talks," and "discussion" techniques for involving youngsters with literature.

Salvatore, Dominic, ed. *The Paperback Goes to School*. New York: Bureau of Independent Publishers and Distributors, 1972. (Out of Print)

In the introduction the editor surveys the history and influence of paperbacks on the school environment. The remainder of the book is a collection of writings by educators who show how the paperback is used as a motivator to interest young people in reading in subject areas such as world literature, social studies, and science.

Smith, Carl B. "Motivating Positive Reading Habits." In *Teaching Reading in Secondary School Content Subjects*, pp. 75-107. New York: Holt, Rinehart, and Winston, 1978.

Smith challenges teachers to recognize the importance of reading attitudes and habits as well as reading ability. He proposes sources of impediments to developing reading attitudes and suggestions for what can be done to remove these. Smith also includes an attitude scale and a book list for further reading.

Smith, James A. *Creative Teaching of Reading in the Elementary School*. 2d ed. Boston: Allyn and Bacon, 1975.

The author surveys the basic principles involved in reading, the nature of reading, teaching of reading, and literature and the reading program. He uses creativity as the basis for the teaching of reading, literature, and poetry to elementary school children.

Sparkman, Brandon and Saul, Jane. *Preparing Your Preschooler for Reading: A Book of Games*. New York: Schocken Books, 1977.

Written primarily for teachers and parents working with preschool children, the work includes numerous suggestions in the form of games to prepare young children for reading. A description of each game with a book list and record list is provided.

Sullivan, George. *A Reason to Read: A Report on an International Symposium on the Promotion of the Reading Habit*. New York: Academy for Educational Development, 1976. (Out of Print)

A report, sponsored by the United States National Commission for UNESCO and conducted by the Academy for Educational Development, reviews the assumptions and questions regarding the purposes of reading, surveys the practical problems of teaching all people to be literate, and sets forth 18 recommendations to promote reading. Especially useful is a list of ten steps in Appendix A titled "A Summary of Ways People Are Motivated to Read."

Thomas, James L. *Turning Kids On to Print Using Nonprint*. Littleton, CO: Libraries Unlimited, 1978.
The author gives specific step-by-step procedures for the production of eight nonprint projects useful in motivating students to read. Detailed information is given on the materials for each project and on the potential costs.

Tierney, Robert J. "Motivating the Superior Reader." *Journal of Research and Development in Education* 11 (1978): 75-79.
Tierney briefly reviews the background research on superior readers, comments on their attitudes and abilities, and then discusses guidelines in the development of superior readers.

Troutner, Joanne. "Tracking Down Readers." *School Library Journal* 24 (March 1978): 106-07.
This is an annotated bibliography of books, films, and filmstrips on car racing as a special interest area. Suggestions are made for introducing the topic along with details such as addresses and prices.

Walker, Jerry L. et al. *Your Reading: A Booklist for Junior High Students*. 5th ed. Urbana, IL: NCTE, 1975.
This annotated book list is divided into subject areas specifically for use by (and with) junior high school students. Reference titles, short story collections, and a list of standard books for all readers are given.

White, Marian F. et al. *High Interest-Easy Reading for Junior and Senior High School Students*. Urbana, IL: NCTE, 1972.
An annotated bibliography of books chosen on the basis that many students will read above their tested reading level if the book has a definite interest appeal. Emphasis is on new books. Arrangement is by subject category.

Wigginton, Eliot, ed. *The Foxfire Book*. Garden City, NY: Anchor Books, 1972, 1973, 1975, 1977.
Foxfire books are collections of the magazines written, illustrated, and produced by the high school students in Rabun Gap, Georgia. The emphasis is on preservation of their culture through oral history. Basically two types of articles are included: "how to do" and interviews with older people in Appalachia.

Zinck, Ann R. and Hawkins, Karla J. "Books for the Reluctant Reader," *Wilson Library Journal* 50 (May 1976): 722-24.
A list of 34 books with brief annotations is given for use with primary through junior high students who are reluctant readers. The criteria for selection are "high interest and ease of readability." Books are divided into subject areas and grade level ranges.

To keep current with new publications in the area of motivational techniques for reading, write to the following addresses for a copy of their current holdings:

Association for Library Service to Children
American Library Association
50 E. Huron Street
Chicago, IL 60611

International Reading Association
800 Barksdale Road
Newark, DE 19711

National Council of Teachers of English
1111 Kenyon Road
Urbana, IL 61801

Young Adult Services Division
American Library Association
50 E. Huron Street
Chicago, IL 60611

Index

Compiled by Joyce A. Post